D1005127

BECOME A PERSON OF
INFLUENCE

Learn basic, fundamental skills to have influence with people and
make a difference in your corporate, family and social life.

BY **GORDON A. MacFARLANE**

Foreword by: **Robert A. Rohm Ph.D.**

Cover art concept: Gordon MacFarlane
Cover artwork and typesetting by: Raweida Khatib
© Copyright   2004 – Gordon MacFarlane
All rights reserved
Romac Communications
Division of 2704146 Canada Incorporated

D.I.S.C. symbols and graphics are trademarks of
Personality Insights Inc., Atlanta Ga.
They are used with their permission.

Second Edition, August 2005

ISBN – 0-9733211-0-5
Printed in the USA

INFLUENCE

In-flu-ence (ín-flu:enze) n. A person's indirect power over men, events or things, e.g. through wisdom, wealth, force of character etc., and not as the exercise of physical force or formal authority - a comparable power in such a thing, *the moon's influence on the tides* - a person or thing having such power - such power to sway authority or people in authority.

In-flu-en-tial (ín-flu:en-chal) adj. Possessing or exerting influence.

QUOTABLE QUOTES

"Iron sharpens iron
so one man sharpens another."
A Proverb of King Solomon

"Success means that you get up
one more time than you fall down."

"Life is like a game of tennis –
you can't win unless you serve well!"

"Teamwork divides the effort
and multiplies the results."

"Whether you think you can or
you think you can't – you're right!"
Henry Ford

"If things go wrong,
don't go with them!"

"People bring sunshine...
some when they come into a room,
others when they leave!"

"In trying times,
don't quit trying!"

"Be quick to listen,
slow to speak and slow to anger."
James, the brother of Jesus

TABLE OF CONTENTS

DEDICATION

To my very best friend and most consistent encourager,
My beautiful wife and life partner, Sandy.
I adore you!

AND

To my four daughters,
Shauna, Amanda, Kristen and Stephanie.

Often, without knowing it, my daughters became like my
very own little lab mice that converted our home into a daily,
real-life laboratory where I was able to experience practical,
hands-on experiences that inspired and "influenced" many
portions of this book.

They are four unique gifts from the Creator.
They are examples of His excellence, and objects
of my affection.

I love you more than you know!

Thanks!

ACKNOWLEDGMENTS

To God, the Master Dreamer who inspired me to dream and
gave me the drive to pursue my dreams!

To "Little Ma", my mom – Shirley MacFarlane,
a real-life angel!

To my late father – Peter MacFarlane,
who modeled a strong work ethic.

To my father-in-law, Bert "U.B." Romandini,
role model, friend and supporter.

To my brother-in-law, Jim McRae,
with his experience, took the time to guide and help me to
create a more understandable and readable product.

To Greg Howard, a good friend who always believed in me and
never gave up on me when many others did.

To Dr. Robert Rohm, my friend and mentor, for his
encouragement and belief. Thank you for the opportunity
to make the completion of this book possible.

To my friend and coach, Mark Wagnon for his belief in me and
his patient, insightful direction.

To Carl Smith, for his always cheerful attitude
and his loyal support.

To my friends, through the years that have positively inspired,
encouraged, led and/or influenced me in their own way...

Bruce Smith	Frank Ryan	Wes Beavis
Lois Andrews	Les Jones	Frank Mikolas
Allan Andrews	Steve Schmidt	Charles Ball
Wylam Price	Bob Chambers	Gord Sutherland
Everett Davis	Mickey Goulet	Denis St-Amour
John Stockhaussen	Dave Smith	Bob Poley
Peter Lamantia	Parker Holman	Joe Kass
Dale Hein	Jean (JJ) Brun	Lloyd Switzer
John McKenna	Chris Simpson	Pierre DesMarais

Thanks!

"Happy is the person who finds wisdom and gains understanding.
For the profit of wisdom is better than the profit of silver, its gain better than that of fine gold."

A Proverb of King Solomon

FOREWORD

I first had the pleasure of meeting Gordon MacFarlane when he attended a Personality Insights training program in Canada. Every time I conduct a certification training seminar, I notice there are different types of individuals in the room. Some attend the training because they want to learn how to get along with other people better. Some attend because they want to use the information at work, school, home or church. Then there are others who develop a passion for sharing the information by coaching, training and helping others. After spending a few days with Gordon, I noticed that he was all of the above! It is fun and exciting for me as a speaker, to have people in the audience like Gordon. As my good friend Les Brown says, "You can tell that there are some people who are "houngry" (hungry)."

After the training was complete, Gordon asked me if it would be possible for him to work on a book project. He explained to me that he wanted to write a book not only about DISC personality information, but also about some ideas he had relating to training, coaching and other information he had been using over the years. I cannot tell you how many times individuals have told me something similar to that. I always reply the same way, "You get all the information together and send it to me and then I will look it over." The reason I do that is because I know 90 percent of the time I will never hear from them again. I know out of my own experience that it is much easier to talk about things than to actually do them. As Yogi Berra once said in his famous quote, "Hard work ain't easy!"

A few months later, I received a manuscript from Gordon. I laughed to myself when I received it, because I thought, "I should have known Gordon was a man of his word and would actually fulfill what he had committed himself to do!" Again, that is because he is "houngry!"

I believe the reader will get much out of this book. There are many helpful concepts that are practical, applicable and useable on a daily basis. I wish Gordon much success in all that he does. I have come to appreciate him as a man who loves and cares about other people and wants to see everyone succeed in all they do.

I would suggest that the reader keep a pen and a notepad handy as he or she reads through this book. Gordon offers many practical ideas and suggestions that everyone will want to implement into his or her daily life. (One good idea can make a major difference in the way you do life.) This book is full of many good ideas that will help you to feel more fulfilled as well as succeed in all you do.

God bless you!

Robert A. Rohm Ph.D.
President, Personality Insights, Inc.
Atlanta, Georgia

INTRODUCTION

Times and people change but principles do not! Success stories and principles have been shared and expressed in many ways. I have been blessed having read many different books that have each, in some way, positively influenced and enhanced my life. The collection of thoughts and principles in this book may not be new to you, but they are timeless and worth hearing again.

As a young person, I was never much of a reader. I started working right out of high school, and it didn't take me long to figure out a couple of things about myself. First, I didn't like taking orders from someone else and second, working for someone else was not going to help me realize my dreams very quickly, like maybe never!

I became determined to find a way to be in business for myself and be my own boss. I worked my way into a few different sales positions and after five very successful years of improving and developing my communication skills and talents, I was hungry for a chance to make it on my own. I ventured into my first business that mercifully only lasted eleven months. That experience taught me some tough but valuable lessons. I had lots of drive, ambition and energy but no real understanding of how to actually build my own company and make it work. I didn't really have anybody to turn to who would direct my drive and help me focus my ambition to make it all come together. I had energy and desire but no solid plan of action and no backup plan. I was learning the hard way. Failure was, unfortunately, inevitable!

I was still green in the world of corporate sales let alone in business ownership, and I was jolted into the frustrating realization that I still had much to learn. The desire and need to be my own boss still lingered, but I knew that I would have to wait until I was better prepared to try again.

With my limited experience and no one to guide me, I decided that I should get some specific training. My strong drive and desire to become successful and lead others prompted me to look to self-help books, audiocassettes and seminars for direction, motivation and inspiration.

I have enjoyed reading books by great and influential people such as Dale Carnegie, Og Mandino, C.S. Lewis, Zig Ziglar, John C. Maxwell, Norman Vincent Peale, Dennis Waitley, Steven Covey, Robert Kiyosaki, and many, many others. (No one book, however, has changed my life more than the Bible. Every success principle I have read in any other book can be traced back to the Bible.) Any book that you read containing life stories, self-help and/or personal development that delivers a benefit to you and extends value to others is a worthwhile investment of your time. Success principles you learn from successful people can and will influence positive change in many different aspects of your life if you allow them to.

Like many of us, I too need to be reminded of the things I should be doing but don't always do. We are all under construction in one way or another. I truly believe that the books you read and the people you choose to associate with will be key factors that influence your values and beliefs. So we must choose wisely! What we focus on and think about the most will ultimately determine the person we will become. We become a product of our environment. I always want to be improving and training myself to be better.

I have come to realize and appreciate that from the training we receive and the skills that we acquire in our youth, each of us will adopt and develop a mannerism for personal communication or what I consider a "personal selling style." Basically, this is the manner in which we communicate and sell who we are to other people in our attempts to connect. Every single day, we sell ourselves in many different ways. We sell our beliefs, our values, our desires, our likes and dislikes. We don't realize we are selling but we actually are. Selling is a form of communication that will lead, persuade or influence people to make a decision or choose a direction.

I believe that a very large part of a person's success in life depends on the degree of influence that he or she possesses in his or her personal selling style.

I began to listen to cassettes instead of music and read books rather than watch television. I would learn through recorded messages and printed pages about how others had achieved and experienced the kind of success I was searching for. I began to see positive and progressive changes in my overall attitude and better results with my focused efforts in sales.

I enrolled in sales training courses and studied books that taught advanced success principles and business skills. My sales career quickly exploded into the top levels of accomplishment and recognition. I ultimately enrolled in a Dale Carnegie sales course to further my development and that opened up a new opportunity for me. Upon completing the course, I was asked to return as a junior instructor and the world of motivational speaking and training was introduced to me. It was a crystal-clear revelation to me that this was my calling. It was something that really excited me and was a professional avenue that I desperately wanted to pursue. It was a new dream to aspire to, and it has since become a passion.

I started to develop my speaking skills part time. While working in my sales career, I began to enjoy success in sales that I had only dreamed about some day accomplishing. In the late 1980's, I decided to start another business with more experience, knowledge and preparation behind me. Today I continue to successfully operate that business and have sprouted two associate businesses as a result of that venture.

The successes I have enjoyed were no mistake! I heard Charlie "Tremendous" Jones once say, "You become the person you are because of the books you read and the people you associate with." This has certainly been true in my life. The books that I have read and the successful people I have chosen to associate with have made an enormous impact in my personal life and in my career. Many authors, speakers and motivators have given me incredible hope and have become my life mentors and teachers. I have reached much higher than I ever would have because of their inspiration, wisdom and encouragement. I am still climbing!

Introduction

If you take ownership and regularly practice the basic people skills and the relationship-building principles that I have packed into this book, you will experience an enormous difference in your ability to sell yourself to others. You will begin to understand yourself and the people around you better by equipping and enabling yourself to build better relationships. If you can develop your people skills to a level where you can consistently communicate hope, encouragement and tolerance, this will guide you to become a person of tremendous influence.

This book is a collection of information, points and some stories that I was led to share. Too many people have regrets in life because they didn't pursue a dream or a desire. I will never have to wonder and ask myself the question that so many ask themselves, "What if?" I did not want to die with this "song" still inside of me. So what's your dream? What's your desire? Don't die with your song still inside of you. Go for it! Woody Allen said, "Ninety percent of success is just showing up." So, here I am!

My hope is that everyone who reads this book will be blessed and influenced in some positive way. From there, your goal should be to pass it on and have a positive impact on someone else. You can leave a legacy of influence and set a standard of excellence.

It's easy material to read, simple to understand and fun to apply. Read on and enjoy learning. I wish you much success and influence!

Cheers!

Gordon MacFarlane
Proverbs 16:3

PEOPLE, PEOPLE, PEOPLE

Out of the billions of people in the world, you need to know and appreciate this fact: you are the only one that ever was and ever will be like you! Look very closely at your fingerprints; understand and recognize this, there is only one person on this whole planet who has those exact prints and that's you! There are no two voice patterns, eye pupil or retina patterns that are exactly alike. That makes you special, unique, a one-of-a-kind! (My wife says "AMEN to that!") You and I have unique and tremendous value, so please don't ever forget that!

In order to increase our influence with others, we have to begin to understand some specific things about people and human nature. We have to realize that there are reasons why people do what they do, say what they say and why they react the way they do under specific conditions. These are known as tendencies, and we are all prone to certain tendencies. Once you learn this, you can begin to skillfully and successfully influence people in many different ways.

To become a good "people person" you must try to recognize and appreciate what unique personality type a person is, so you can understand, adjust and position yourself to be more relatable. What that really means is that you need to identify what their specific behavior tendencies may be. When you know these details about someone, you can be more understanding and tolerant of behavior and attitudes that present themselves in that person. This will often maximize the depth and longevity of your relationship together.

The essential starting point for incredible influence with others is to discover who you are and which personality blend you possess. This will be your first assignment! This will empower you and enable you to clearly identify with who you actually are and how you have been "wired." This information will help you to better understand yourself and allow you to better understand others in order to build stronger relationships.

Personalities - Where it all started

Without getting too detailed, I am going to simply try to show you that each person has a primary or dominant personality style that is complemented by a blend of three other personality types. These four styles make up our unique behavioral tendencies. This is the very distinct and predictable way that people filter information that helps them to think, feel, act or respond. The way in which they view life through these "filters" will establish a behavioral style, which we refer to as a personality style. Your personal behavioral tendency may be very similar to someone else but it will rarely be identical.

Personality information is not new. As early as approximately 400 B.C., Hippocrates, the father of modern medicine, established the "Four Behavioral Style" approach to understanding people. His theory was that the predominance of certain bodily fluids, like phlegm (pronounced flem) and bile, that a person possessed, determined the temperament or personality type of that person. Some people were identified as highly assertive and others were low in assertive behavior. Some were very responsive and others were not so responsive. So, Hippocrates named these temperaments after the bodily fluids that he believed influenced their behavior. The terms choleric, sanguine, phlegmatic and melancholy are still in use today, even though we have long since understood that our bodily fluids do not determine our behavior and our disposition.

In the 1920's, Dr. William Marston, a Columbia University psychologist, identified four major patterns of behavior that are present in everyone to a greater or lesser degree. In 1928, he published his findings in a book entitled *Emotions of Normal People*. His theory and teachings were based on the "D.I.S.C." model of human behavior. I believe the "D.I.S.C." model is the easiest understood and taught model on human behavior.

2

Today, Dr. Robert Rohm of Personality Insights in Atlanta Georgia, has taken the research of Dr. Marston's D.I.S.C. model to a new level. Recent publications by Dr. Rohm, further simplify this information, so that most individuals can grasp it quickly and then easily communicate it to others. I will be using the D.I.S.C. model in this book, because I believe it is the easiest model to understand. The first chapter of this book contains powerful ideas and principles based on the D.I.S.C model found in Dr. Rohm's books and in his teachings. Within each chapter, I will attempt to connect individual people skills with each of the unique personalities in order to provide a clearer understanding to help increase your influence.

The goal for this portion of the book is to help you identify:
- What your personality style blend is
- What your predominant single trait is
- What your secondary trait is
- What your specific drive motor tendency is
- What your orientation that will steer your tendency is

Illustration Blend of the Old and New

The titles for the Four Behavioral Styles of Hippocrates and Dr. William Marston's D.I.S.C. method are compared in the list below. I have added the "Primary Desire" of each of the personalities in an attempt to make it easier for you to understand and apply to today's reality.

400 BC Hippocrates		1920 - Dr. Marston Personality Type		Primary Desire
Choleric	(koe-LAIR-ik)	'D'	DOMINANT	Power
Sanguine	(SAAN-gwin)	'I'	INFLUENCING	Recognition
Phlegmatic	(fleg-MAT-ik)	'S'	SUPPORTIVE	Harmony
Melancholy	(MEL-on-kol-e)	'C'	CAUTIOUS	Perfection

3

Research tells us that the joys and victories as well as the stresses and tensions that we experience in our lives will cause us to fall into very predictable patterns of behavior. This research is a bridge of discovery into the unique differences in people, so we can understand each other better and build better relationships. The research helps us gain valuable information like what our ideal environment is for promoting maximum results and what our basic needs are for improving long-term survival and happiness.

We also know from this research that everyone is a blend of the four types. The four different styles weave together in amazing ways. Knowing how to use the blends in a complementary fashion is the secret to success.

Principle: Understand that we are all different with a purpose.

The goal and intent of providing this information is not to determine which personality type is right or wrong or who is better or worse, good or bad. It's just to point out quite simply that we are all different. We should never stop making the effort to climb to a higher level of understanding, so we can get along better with others, accomplish more and enjoy life to the fullest. Knowledge is power!

"Use power to help people. For we are given power not to advance our own purposes, nor to make a great show in the world, nor a name. There is but one just use of power and it is to serve people."
George Bush, Sr.

THE FOUR MAIN PERSONALITY TYPES

Are you Outgoing or Reserved?

Each of us has an "internal motor" that drives us. It has a fast pace that makes us more outgoing, or it has a slow pace that makes us more reserved. Basically, this is what powers us and determines the degree of intensity that we put into all the things we do. Everyone knows a person who is fast-paced and energetic, and everyone knows a person who is slow-paced and laid-back. One is not better than the other. They are just different. We need both types of people to make life happen and create a balance. This is a good starting point to begin discovering who we really are.

Outgoing People

Outgoing people are the fast-paced types who do everything at full speed. They seem to always be going somewhere and going in a hurry! They think, speak, eat, move and even sleep fast. They are optimistic, positive thinkers with little concern for details. They are very good at seeing the big picture. They are very energetic and possess a perpetual can-do attitude.

Outgoing people are enthusiastic and expect positive results from all of their endeavors. They are usually involved in community projects, civic clubs and all kinds of organizations where they often hold leadership positions. They like being in charge of things where they can be a "director" and tell people what to do. The things they do and how they look tend to be very important to them.

Reserved People

The reserved, laid-back or slow-paced person casually strolls along through life and takes everything in. They like to savor a meal, enjoy the ride and take in the view. They delight in the process of most endeavors.

They can be generally personified by the words "steady," "predictable" and "reliable." They usually get tired just looking at or thinking about an outgoing, fast-paced person. They can be classified as too methodical, selective and boring. Some are very analytical and quickly see things for what they really are. They are also very patient and have great stamina to see things through to completion. Most of them are not talkative, instead, they prefer listening. They are generally not initiators but will wrap things up nicely.

Reserved individuals are concerned about the details of a situation before doing something, because they do not like to be surprised. They would prefer to have a safe plan rather than take things as they come. They tend to be more passive and would rather be a spectator than a player. They would much prefer to operate behind the scenes rather than in the spotlight.

The circle at the right illustrates these two types of people and their specific motor activity. They are both equally important and of equal value. We need both types to make life work!

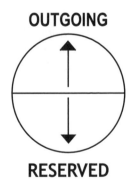

OUTGOING

RESERVED

Are you Task-Oriented or People-Oriented?

We must now concern ourselves with the direction in which we are drawn toward. Like the magnetic pull of a compass, we are either prone to tasks or to people. In the last section, you probably identified with one of the drive activities more than the other. It will be the same for this section; you will be naturally drawn to one of these two orientations illustrated below.

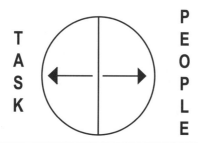

Task-Oriented People

Think of the well-oiled, super-charged, firing-on-all-cylinders, fine-tuned running machine. That's task-oriented people. Task-oriented people find great pleasure in a job well done. We like to call them high tech. Function is important to them. They like to make things work. They have intense focus on getting things done. Accomplishing things is what they love. They are planners. They enjoy seeing a plan come together, and their plans generally work.

This group is so focused on the tasks at hand that they easily ignore the feelings of others. Important relationship skills are sometimes missing in these individuals. They care deeply about people, but they do not always show it. They frequently give off signals that people are bothering them.

7

People-Oriented People

The obvious orientation here is people! They love to visit and chat and not necessarily with someone they know. They love to interact. You can consider these types the touchy, feely kind of people. They are into caring and sharing with others. Being with people energizes them. Life to them is all about being with people. Moreover, they want to make sure that what they are doing or saying doesn't offend people. They want to be included and liked. They love to be invited to do social things.

Sometimes their social orientation causes them to delay or decrease productivity. They are easily drawn away from tasks by the opportunity to have conversations with others. They naturally let their feelings rather than their mind, control them. This can cause them to make unwise decisions.

Bringing it all together

What we end up with is four distinct types, like four pieces of a pie. The pieces become interconnected in an amazing way. Together with D.I.S.C., they make up the many diverse blends and combinations of personalities that are who we are, the human race.

At this point, you are probably getting an idea of the kind of person you are. These preferences will vary in degree and intensity in people. No one is 100 percent task-oriented or 100 percent people-oriented, just like no one is 100 percent outgoing or 100 percent reserved. We all have a blend of a drive motor and a specific orientation as shown in the illustration. Remember, one of these drive motors or orientations is not better than the other, just different.

Outgoing people are more active and optimistic. They keep us moving forward to new things. Reserved people are more passive and cautious. They keep us from taking too many risks and making too many changes too fast.

We can learn the differences of each style as a foundation for change to become balanced than we are now. We can also use this information to become more influential in the lives of other people. Before we bring **D.I.S.C.** together with these four quadrants, let's look at some ways that we can potentially make adjustments to how and why we do things.

To become a person of influence...

The outgoing, fast-paced types will want to learn how to become more calculated, careful and steady to bring more balance to their personality. They can learn to slow down and take a breather!

The reserved, slow-paced types will bring more balance to their personality by learning how to be more demanding and interactive. They can learn to rise up out of your seat, move around and get more involved and don't keep to yourself as much.

Task-oriented people will add some balance to their personality by learning to enjoy the process of their efforts. Also they can try to remember that people have feelings. They can learn to become more involved in conversations by listening more intently and smiling like they mean it!

People-oriented people need to try and stay focused on the things they start and try to finish one or two of them. Try to establish an agenda, and stick to it. Take a moment to plan your work, and then work your plan.

We are all different...
- Some people see the glass half full, others half empty.
- Some people are ambitious; some people are complacent.
- Some people are direct, dominant and determined.
- Some people are submissive, reserved and laid-back.

Are you a 'D,' an 'I,' an 'S' or a 'C'? Let's put the pieces together and find your specific, most predominate trait that makes you – you!

We see that:

THE **D** TYPE IS OUTGOING AND TASK-ORIENTED.
THE **I** TYPE IS OUTGOING AND PEOPLE-ORIENTED.
THE **S** TYPE IS RESERVED AND PEOPLE-ORIENTED.
THE **C** TYPE IS RESERVED AND TASK-ORIENTED.

Summary of Illustration: How the **D.I.S.C.** letters tie in together is the key to remembering the **D.I.S.C.** model of human behavior.

The top half of the circle shows the 'D' and 'I' personalities that are both outgoing or fast-paced, but they have different motivational drives. The 'D' or dominant personality on the top left side wants to put energy into getting the job done which identifies them as more task-oriented.

The 'I', or inspiring type, top right, wants to put all energy into having fun while achieving acceptance and recognition for their accomplishments; there must be an element of enjoyment. This identifies them as more people-oriented.

The bottom half of the circle shows that the 'S' and 'C' personalities are both reserved or slow-paced, but they possess different motivational drives. The 'C', or cautious personality, on the bottom left, will focus on getting the job done with perfection in a specific time frame, which identifies them as more task-oriented. The 'S', or supportive personality, on the bottom left, has a desire to be friendly with as many people as possible and not offend anyone. This, along with a slow-paced, easygoing approach to life identifies them as being more people-oriented.

'D' Type Personality – Dominant
Outgoing and Task-oriented

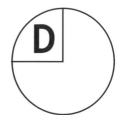

(Hippocrate's - Choleric):
Top left of circle
These people like to be in charge.

Color Green: Green light means all systems are GO!
! symbol depicts the '**D**' type, because they are emphatic in everything! Get the job done – just do it! That's a '**D**'!

Some key words to describe strengths of this personality:

Dominant, **D**irect, **D**emanding, **D**etermined, **D**ecisive, **D**river and **D**o it now. **Other Strengths:** Strong - willed, Adventuresome, Practical, Productive, Confident, Star Performer, Problem solver, Take charge, Conqueror, Stick-to-itiveness, Thick skinned, Powerful.

For the '**D**' personality, nothing beats a challenging situation. They are pioneers and adventurers who want to go faster, farther and deeper than others have gone. They love to be in charge and direct the group. They are dynamic leaders. The 'D' type is ambitious and strong-willed and seems to thrive on pressure. They are very competitive and always want to win. They will always give that extra effort, if that's what it takes.

High '**D**' types are very demanding of themselves and others and will seldom take *no* for an answer. They are direct in their approach to handling problems. Empathy is not their strong suit, and they are often blunt and to the point with their words. If you want a direct answer, ask a '**D**'.

'**D**' types are bottom-line people with not much use for details. They are both determined and independent. When others feel defeated and want to quit, they are courageous. They will persevere in the face of adversity. Since they are persistent, a "no" to them means "maybe later."

11

'**D**' Type Personality (continued)

The '**D**' type is wired to handle the heat and the pressure and thrives on it. They can make the hard decisions in hard times.

Some weaknesses you need to be aware of:
Domineering, Defiant, Dictator, Determined, Dogmatic, Dictatorial, Arrogant, Insensitive, Impatient, Sarcastic, Pushy, Strong-willed, Unemotional, Offensive, Conceited, Abrasive, Cold, Cruel, Inconsiderate, Proud.

You won't get much sympathy from '**D**' type people, and that may make them seem cold and uncaring. A '**D**' personality sees the need for sympathy as a sign of weakness, and they would never want to appear weak. In addition, they are quick to answer and their lack of thinking may make them appear rude and reckless. '**D**' types are excellent at behind-the-scenes manipulation and sometimes they work with hidden agendas. Their confidence can be mistaken for cockiness.

'**D's**' love to win. They love to win so much that they can become ruthless in their quest to dominate. It's not about how to play the game; it's about how to win! Winning at all costs can often permanently damage relationships. This can be avoided with some sensitivity and patience towards other players. '**D's**' have to be careful about their short fuse and hot temper. Interestingly, they do have an ability to forgive, forget and move on faster than any other personality. It's "history" to them. Forget it and let's move on!

Our Determined '**D**' individuals – Making their mark...
The '**D**' personality types make excellent producers and builders and leaders in any field. They make great coaches and military officers. They are good teachers, preachers, police officers, political leaders and corporate leaders. They make good criminals too. They want to move and shake the world and usually do.

Approximately 10% of the population shares this profile.

'I' Type Personality - Inspiring
Outgoing and People - oriented

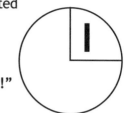

(Hippocrate's - Sanguine):
Top right of circle
These people like to have fun. "Let's Party!"

Color Red: Red is FIERY, exciting and bright. **STOP**; watch me!
★ symbol depicts the 'I' type, because they love to be the star of
the show, up front and center stage.

Some key words to describe strengths of this personality:
Inspiring, Influencing, Impressionable, Interactive, Impulsive,
Impressive, Initiators, Interesting, Imaginative and Involved.
Other Strengths: Talkative, Energetic, Charming, Warm, Friendly,
Persuasive, Transparent, Center of attention, Enthusiastic,
Outgoing, Bright, Life of the party, Spontaneous.

High 'I's' are so impulsive that they will say *yes* before you
complete your question if it starts with "Do you want to go?" They
like to be on the move or do anything if there is fun involved.
They are energy personified. They want to enjoy everything life
has to offer. They love to stir things up and get the party started.
Generally, they **are** the party!

The high 'I' type can meet a total stranger and feel right at home
with them. They never really want to be grown up or take life too
seriously. They have a great sense of humor and love to laugh.
They have a positive and optimistic disposition that makes them
fun to be around. 'I's' don't stay mad for long, because after all
life is too short. In addition, they work very well with others.

Recognition and approval are strong basic needs for the high 'I'
personality. They are very friendly and carefree, and they often
exhibit more confidence in themselves than ability. They are very
creative and persuasive. 'I's' are very good at expressing their
ideas.

13

'I' Type Personality (continued)

Some weaknesses you need to be aware of:
Impetuous, Impulsive, Illogical, Inconsistent, Inability to focus, Talkative, Risk-taker, Restless, Emotional, Loud, Exaggerates, Easily tempted, Weak-willed, Egocentric, Undependable, Can't keep secrets, Not good finishers.

Although high 'I's' are optimistic and will use that to encourage others, they can carry that to an extreme and become unrealistic. They will tend to ignore important facts and not face reality. This will cause them to lose credibility with others. The 'I' personalities are good with words and stories. They are so good at making things appear like no-lose propositions, that they can make things sound better than they actually are. They will sometimes take storytelling to a manipulative level in order to get you to see their point of view. High 'I's' that follow a consistent pattern of this kind of communication can make great con artists, because they seem so believable. This can cause deep hurt, resentment and even destroy relationships.

Because high 'I's' are so spontaneous, they can easily become impulsive. They can jump to another exciting opportunity and then another without first producing any tangible results from their first endeavor. They have trouble with focusing their energy and seeing a task to its completion. In addition, their excitement can become uncontrolled emotion and cause outbursts of impatience and anger.

Our Inspiring 'I' individuals – Making their mark...
They make excellent actors, motivational speakers, salespeople and comedians. They're good personal friends. They make a great disc jockey, announcer, auctioneer and clown. If talking is the main focus they should excel!

Approximately 30% of the population shares this profile.

'S' Type Personality - Supportive
Reserved and People - oriented

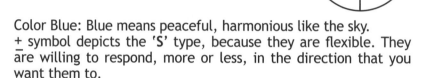

(Hippocrate's - Phlegmatic):
Bottom right of circle
These people like to be appreciated.

Color Blue: Blue means peaceful, harmonious like the sky.
± symbol depicts the 'S' type, because they are flexible. They
are willing to respond, more or less, in the direction that you
want them to.

Some key words to describe strengths of this personality:
Supportive, Steady, Sentimental, Sweet, Secure, Stable, Shy,
Self-sacrificing, Systematic and Status quo. **Other Strengths:**
Loyal, Very Patient, Easygoing, Polite, Meek, Reserved,
Appreciative, Reliable, Not pushy, Trustworthy, Observant,
Nice, Conservative, Diplomatic, Humorous, Quiet, Calm, Good
finishers, Good listeners, Hate conflict, Hate confrontation.

The 'S' types are labeled as steady, because they are so even-
tempered and reliable. They have a warm heart and love being
at home with one or two close friends sipping cocoa. They don't
handle pressure well at all and prefer things to stay routine with
no changes in their pattern. 'S's' feel secure when things are
running smoothly. They will easily adapt to any situation and fit
in for fear of being noticed. They will avoid being put in the
spotlight and would much prefer working behind the scenes in a
supporting role.

The 'S' personality will have a difficult time saying *no,* and they
will struggle against being forceful with someone. They are
excellent team players even though they are naturally passive
and shy. This style will enjoy having fun with people as long as
the fun isn't centered around them. They are quiet, back-seat
dwellers and will do nothing to purposely oppose you. They want
you to like them. They really don't want to ruffle any feathers.
'S's' are great at keeping secrets, forever if need be.

'S' Type Personality (continued)

The 'S' is the most loyal of friends and will want to serve the people closest to them and meet their needs. They are trustworthy, dependable and model listeners. They bring comfort and stability to relationships, because they have a relaxed and easygoing demeanor. They are also predictable.

Some weaknesses you need to be aware of:
Stubborn, Selfish, Stingy, Sucker, Indecisive, Fearful, Lazy, Too patient, People pleasers (afraid to say *no*), Overcautious, Timid, Easily taken advantage of, Not good initiators, Not risk takers, Too dependant.

'S' people are so practical and indecisive that they may miss out on excellent opportunities. They often appear to have a lack of initiative. They much prefer to take things slowly and even stick with the status quo rather than consider another alternative. This all stems from not really liking change. They are resistant to change and can be quite stubborn. If there is a chance of failure, 'S' individuals would prefer to do nothing. 'S's' are caring and cooperative people. They are softhearted. They will work with people and go the extra mile when others won't. They will sacrifice their own needs for others even at a loss. They need to toughen up and learn to say *no* sometimes!

'S' types can hold a grudge by keeping something that bothers them deep inside and harbor long-term resentment. They prefer to say nothing for fear of hurting the person who may have hurt them first. They are very uncomfortable with confrontation.

Our steady 'S' individuals – Making their mark...
'S' type people make excellent secretaries, nurses and technicians, because they are very people-oriented. They're good personal friends. They make good accountants, bankers and business administrators. They make great counselors. 'S's' enjoy helping others.

Approximately 35% of the population shares this profile.

'C' Type Personality – Cautious
Reserved and Task - oriented

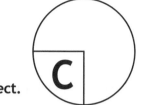

(Hippocrate's - Melancholy):
Bottom left of circle
These people like quality and being correct.

Color Yellow: A yellow light, means **CAUTION**, move carefully!
? symbol depicts the **'C'** type, because they love to question everything. They seek clarification.

Some key words to describe strengths of this personality:
Cautious, Calculated, Careful, Critical thinkers, Competent, Curious, Conscientious and Conformists. **Other Strengths:** Organized, Precise, Detailed, Logical, Punctual, Perfectionist, Patient, Intellectual, Orderly, Business-like, Neat, Traditional.

'C's' external appearance is a statement of internal condition. That's why they are neat fanatics. They love clear documentation and accurate information. They are very seldom wrong, because they have double-checked everything. They take mistakes, when pointed out, very personally.

High 'C' types are very analytical and will painstakingly break down each of their projects into workable components and complete each one in order until the entire task is done. While they do tend to get slowed down with details, high 'C's' will often see pitfalls that other styles may overlook and ultimately be more structured and productive as a result of their high standards.

'C's' love consistency, because it creates a familiar comfort zone in which they can function. They are also very tenacious and hard working and can be counted on for quality work even if it means extra hours. 'C's' are fanatics about doing things by the book and will seem rebellious or disrespectful when they continue to ask questions when assigned a specific task. They need clarification and complete understanding, so they don't mess up. 'C' types want to look the best and be the best.

17

'**C**' Type Personality (continued)

Some weaknesses you need to be aware of:
Critical, Unsociable, Negative, Rigid nature, Self-centered, Moody, Faultfindering, Impractical, Overcautious, Vengeful, Superiority complex, Know-it-all, Not risk takers, Indecisive, Worrisome, Easily discouraged, Party-poopers, Too detailed.

If you have made a mistake with '**C**'s', they are not afraid to inform you; it's their duty and you should know! "Do it right or don't do it at all," is their motto. However, telling it like it is may not win them many friends. They tend to believe they are always right, and as a result, display an air of self-centeredness. This could cause them to appear unsociable. Because most of life is a serious game, they have little time for nonsense. '**C**' people are driven to a standard of perfection, and this can cause others to feel they are just critical of any other standard. High '**C**'s' are able to focus with great intensity. The whole world could be crashing in around them, and they would be hard at work at their station, completing the task. They can often be very rigid.

'**C**'s' are so curious about getting all the facts, they could be seen as nosey. They are deep thinkers - much more that any of the other personalities. Because they are so detailed and precise, they can be picky. While '**C**'s' are usually correct about what they find, most people don't want to know that much about things. '**C**' individuals do not generally let their emotions show and expects others to do the same. They prefer answers that are based on clear and irrefutable facts, not emotional responses.

Our cautious '**C**' individuals – Making their mark...
The '**C**' personality types make excellent teachers, researchers, scientists and inventors. They are often good investors, accountants and bookkeepers. '**C**'s' make good philosophers, artists and musicians. They are also great marathon runners.

Approximately 25% of the population shares this profile.

More influence understanding and applying D.I.S.C.

When I went through certification training with Dr. Robert Rohm on understanding personalities, one of the most important things I learned was that the goal is understanding "who" we are not to label each other, not to criticize people, or put people in a box. The goal is to understand people...yourself and others, so we can all get along better.

Successful people have one thing in common: they will seek knowledge from the best possible source in order to grow in understanding and wisdom. As we understand people and what drives them, we realize that it's all about self-interest. People don't do things against you, rather they will do things for themselves. It's a "me first" world that we live in. Try not to take it personally; just understand it, and work with it.

Here are some final thoughts and suggestions that may help and encourage you to initiate change, so you can influence others. These are presented to you in this way to challenge you to adjust, change and grow. They are not meant to offend you but provoke you to think. Our strengths make us who we are but taken to extremes, they can become a liability to us. Just remember this: it's all about learning balance.

To help increase influence as a '**D**':

'**D's**' are usually all business, and they are good at it - sometimes to a fault! Business is all they want to do! The action-driven '**D**' needs to slow down and take some time to check out finer details they may be missing as they move boldly from task to task. Stop, relax and smell the flowers! '**D**' people enjoy achievement and will pursue a relationship if they are accomplishing things with those involved. If you're a '**D**', pause for a moment and understand that you don't have to do something just to get results. You can do things for the fun of it! I know you may be thinking, "Why?!", but just try it. While yoga may be too much to ask of a high '**D**', just try to sit still somewhere and enjoy the scenery. Loosen up; read a novel.

19

To help increase influence as an 'D': (continued)

'D's' should try to keep away from the things that stress them, because when stressed, they get very angry. Physical activity, like walking or swimming, helps relieve some of their stress. High 'D' individuals should try to see things from the other person's perspective more often. Learning how to get along with others and becoming a little more personable and sensitive will help their cause. 'D' people might do well to learn how to show some emotion for something or someone. This will assure others that they are not all "machine" and that they do have a human side to them. I tell 'D's' to try not to run over people. The world needs the 'D' types to get things done, but they need to bring some people along. We are referred to as the human race, not just the race!

To help increase influence as an 'I':

'I' individuals are naturally influential to most people. They can inspire people to action with their can-do spirit and boundless energy. 'I's' can light up a room by simply walking into it. They typically are in good humor and always in search of the next "good time." They are fun but often to a fault. Humor is a great gift and can be a strength, but they may not know when to stop being funny or having "fun." Controlling their emotions and excitement and understanding timing will help them, because too much energy has a tendency to overwhelm most people and turn them off.

Time management is a big struggle for 'I' people, so an agenda is a great idea as long as they use it for more than just a phone book! They would be wise to select an inexpensive one, because they may misplace it a few times. If an 'I' type person can get serious about consistently using an agenda, this will be a major breakthrough in helping them remain on track to achieve goals.

To help increase influence as an 'I': (continued)

A big challenge for the impatient 'I' types is **FOCUS!** Multitasking is not safe for them. It is imperative that they focus on one thing at a time. They will feel very good when they accomplish something. They must be cautious and control their excitement, because every task completed is not necessarily a reason to celebrate. Stay the course, keep going!

They must focus and concentrate on listening to the person who is talking rather than wanting to eagerly share what they have to say. A good drill for 'I's' is to practice keeping eye contact as part of their quest to learn focus. They will have to fight the urge to keep their radar on full alert in their attempts to hear all of the other conversations that may be happening within earshot. People are important to an 'I', and they need friendly relations to keep them going, but if they do not take the time to show that they appreciate people by listening to what they are saying, they will be a very lonely people person. For an 'I' type, being alone is not enjoyable. 'I' personalities are very likeable and will be people of tremendous influence if they are able to listen better and be more consistent. They must be careful in their conversations to choose the right time and place to use humor.

To help increase influence as an 'S':

An 'S' personality has to be reassured that saying *no* is all right! They are so focused on the well - being of others that they will sacrifice their own comfort for others. This is amplified if they are friends because of the loyalty they feel towards a companion. 'S's' will grow in courage and influence if they clearly understand that there is a potential opportunity in every change.

Overcoming fear is one of the biggest obstacles for the 'S' personality. If they can remember an acronym for fear, it will help. It is: False Evidence Appearing Real. 'S's' need to boldly move forward in faith, and not be paralyzed by the fear of the unknown or what may never be.

21

To help increase influence as an 'S': (continued)

The 'S' personality has a genuine fear of looking bad in front of others and the potential embarrassment that goes with it. They must get used to the fact that failure and the occasional embarrassment is all a part of learning *and* to learn is to grow.

The 'S' person must be willing to take a few risks in life and do something that is completely out of character. I suggest they wear a bright color and get noticed! By the way, powder blue is not a bright color! A bright yellow or orange or fiery red is what I'm talking about! I know, the high 'S' can't believe I am even suggesting such a thing. It's almost personality cleansing.

'S' individuals must be made aware that being very predictable, boring and dull never influenced people to change. Just once, 'S's' should try not knowing where they're going or what they're doing and feel like a reckless, crazy kid! They are convinced that other people will hate them and think they are silly. Take the 'D' approach, "Who cares what someone thinks; just do it!" It is not always important to do the next right thing. Run through a fountain with an 'I' person, arm wrestle with a 'D' and hide the lunch of a 'C'. It really doesn't matter what people think. Have some high-powered enjoyment and get out of your comfort zone! Be different from your standard beige or vanilla! Be a fruity, zesty, tangy flavor! Break free have some fun!

To help increase influence as an 'C':

High 'C' people are some of the most knowledgeable and smart people on the planet, because they seek details and information. Their desire for perfection and complete clarity of things makes them a tad too serious for most people. They need to try to smile more - much more. I have several suggestions for 'C's': Relax and have some fun. Live a little! Stand in an ankle - deep puddle with shoes on. You don't always have to understand everything. Sing at a karaoke bar - without the words. Reckless? Preposterous? (Maybe! But go crazy anyway!)

To help increase influence as an '**C**': (continued)

The '**C**' style tends to lack faith, because everything has to be proven to them. They have to be aware that thorough explanations are not always possible. They need to trust that they will not be lost or useless if they do not have all the information. The need to exercise faith in something and take a risk.

'**C's**' have to learn to put the emphasis on people and not so much on the process and the task. People have value and play an important part in the success of the projects of the '**C's**'. If '**C's**' want to have influence, they will need to at least acknowledge people are present and have significance!

High '**C**' personalities need to be reassured that it's okay to make a mistake. They need to learn not to punish themselves and others for the mistakes that do occur. It is important for them to control what they can control and don't worry about what they cannot control. People wired as high '**C's**' must remember the human factor. The value of people does not come from what they know, but who they are. We are human beings not human doings!

Conclusion

The details covered in these first pages of this book give you only a basic understanding of the **D.I.S.C.** model of human behavioral styles. There is much more to learn and understand about personalities, such as the different blends and environmental tendencies, graphing your style and much, much more. Just remember, while each of us has a dominant style, we are a blend of all four styles. The individual letters are meant to be objective and descriptive rather than subjective and judgmental.

In the up-coming chapters, I will provide you with specific people skills to grow your influence with others. I will show you how each one of the **D.I.S.C.** personalities can connect to these skills for explosive and influential results.

"People are always blaming their circumstances for what they are. I don't believe in circumstances. The people who get ahead in this world are the people who get up and look for the circumstances they want, and if they can't find them, make them."

George Bernard Shaw

2

ATTITUDE AND PROGRAMMING

"As a man thinks in his heart, so is he!"
A Proverb of King Solomon

A positive attitude is essential for someone who wants to be a person of influence. A positive attitude is seeing things from the plus side of life. For example, a positive person will see a glass filled with fluid to half its capacity as always half full not half empty. Every day is a great day, no matter what the weather. The majority of their thoughts and comments promote good cheer and optimism. This is a result of specific and proper programming of their attitude. An optimistic attitude towards all things is a decision they've made.

A positive attitude will empower you to do everything with passion. To have passion is to have a strong feeling or powerful desire for something. You can always tell when someone has a passion for something; they approach it with energy and positive determination.

Most high "I" type personalities do things with a flare and passion! They seem to have a perpetually good attitude about most things. It is the only way they would choose to do something, and it comes naturally. Each of the other personalities might try and follow the lead of our high-energy 'I' friends and enjoy life as they do!

The 'D', 'C' and 'S' types can and will do things with a proper attitude but for the right reasons. Basically, having a proper attitude requires some thought for these personality types. The biggest factor is what they're telling themselves, because that's what programs them. The high 'D' needs to be accomplishing something to feel good. High 'C' individuals like to justify everything including why they should be positive and optimistic, because that's not their natural response. There must be a good reason. The 'S' will have a calm, and easy approach to everything. If being positive will make you happy, they will change and be happy too. If you're happy, I'm happy!

For every person, the type of thoughts and comments that program their mind is the key to the attitude they will possess. The ways in which they speak and act are the influential results. A proverb of King Solomon states, "You will become what you dwell on and think upon most." Think positive and upbeat thoughts and your attitude and actions will generally reflect those same thoughts.

There is an attractive energy in a positive attitude, and people can feel it when they are around you. You give from what you have! The other side of the story is that there is an energy that surrounds a negative attitude also. That energy unfortunately makes it very uncomfortable for people to be around. It's very real and not very attractive!

Allow me to share an experience I had one day in a department store elevator. I was the third person to get onto this elevator on a middle floor that was headed to the lower level. The only other passengers from the upper floor were an elderly man and a much younger man who I recognized by his clothing to be an employee of the store.

As the door began closing, the young employee stopped it to allow two other passengers to enter. I noticed right away that the elderly man was not pleased by this action and obviously viewed it as an unnecessary delay. As the door began to close a second time a young mother politely called out to stop the door from closing as she pushed her stroller quickly towards the opening. The young man obliged and stopped the door's progress so she could enter. Upon doing so, two other young girls scurried in behind her and giggled like they just sneaked on for a free ride at the fairground and melodically said, "Thank-you." A shy, "No problem," was the young clerk's reply as he released the door, so it could close and begin our descent to the lower level. I smiled to myself and thought this was a kind and considerate young person, who had the heart of a server! When the door finally closed, the elderly man hurled a comment at him I never expected to hear after such a great display of kindness by a young person.

Casting a glare at the young lad, the elderly man snapped crisply, "If you keep doing that for everyone, we'll be here all day, YOU JERK!" Those poisonous words affected everyone in the enclosure. His comments were an injustice to proper human behavior. He should have been ashamed.

The young man, never losing his smile made no reply and chose to look away from him and then down at the floor. Everyone on the elevator could feel the ugliness of the comment and the negative attitude of that elderly man. He should have applauded the kind gestures displayed by this young man. I was very disappointed with the older man. I noticed the etched scowl that reflected his sour attitude. It was written all over his face, as he glared at the young lad in anger for the duration of the ride.

The descent of only one floor seemed to take much longer than it did. The people on the elevator seemed happy when the elevator doors opened, and they were finally able to free themselves from the quiet, nervous energy that loomed in that tight compartment because of someone's bad attitude.

Being the last one to leave the elevator, I fired off a smile and a wink at the young man, and he shrugged his shoulders and smiled back and said, "What are you going to do but smile eh?" Luckily, that unfortunate and negative experience did not change the young man's outlook. I believe it was because of two things: how he was wired and the programming of his attitude. His right attitude kept everything in perspective.

This experience was a stark reminder that **our attitude** can mean the difference between making or breaking someone's day! We all need to work very hard to keep our attitude on the positive side of the ledger, and we will attract people to us and not repel them. Program your attitude for positive influence.

It is not the situation, but the way we respond to the situation that's important.

When you decide to change your attitude regarding your life and the relationships you have, it will make a dramatic difference in your life and in your relationships.

You and you alone will decide what will ultimately program the most powerful computer known to mankind. It's your very own personal computer, your mind. What you read, what you listen to and what you confess with your mouth will etch the programs of your mind and memory. This will play and replay for you whenever you need to resource it.

In the computer world, there is an oft-used expression, "garbage in, garbage out" which is very accurate. But the opposite is also true in that if you put good stuff in, you'll get the good stuff out. It is the same with people. It is about reaping what you sow. That's why we tell our children to be careful with whom they associate. I always tell my kids, "Be the one who's being the positive influence, not the one who's being influenced to do wrong."

"Remember, happiness doesn't depend upon who you are or what you have; it depends solely upon what you think."
Dale Carnegie

Every one of the four main personalities can be positively influential if they adopt and practice a "praise and promote" attitude. Praise people for their actions and acts of kindness. Promote the strengths and the things you admire in people. Praise and compliment people and see how many faces you can light up with a smile. Make a goal to compliment at least one person you don't know every day. What a great goal!

This may require an attitude adjustment if this is not a normal practice for you. But what incredible results you will have. It takes 21 days to form a habit, so start today with your attitude program change and do not miss a day. If you miss a day, you must start over. After 21 days of the same activity, it will become a regular part of your life.

If you will practice these points for 21 days, they will help you create winning habits and maintain a positive attitude:

1. Read motivational, inspiring and positive material for at least 15 - 30 minutes a day.
2. Listen to and re-listen to recorded messages or music that feeds the mind with motivation, inspiration and positive information.
3. Associate with positive, upbeat people who have goals and dreams and want to accomplish great things in life.

So, confess what you want to have. Write it down, set a date and plan your work then work your plan. It's a simple process and it's easy to apply if you say so! If you say it's hard, it will be. The mind is very powerful and will believe what you program it to believe. Success is a decision! If you have the attitude that you will succeed, then you will! It's just a question of when.

Your standard should be for excellence in everything you do. Settle for nothing less! If you can't do it with excellence, then don't do it. At least make the effort for excellence even if the results aren't excellent. What if your goal is average and you miss and fall short? With a focus on achieving excellence you'll always land above average. You will also feel much better knowing that you gave it all you were capable of giving. If you were to ask my children, "What's your dad's favorite word?" I am confident they would tell you, rolling their eyes simultaneously, "Excellence!"

One thousand people with only an interest are no match for a single person with a positive attitude, a commitment to an action plan and a standard of excellence.

"If you can dream it, you can do it."
Walt Disney

If we think back to the first chapter, I talked about fingerprints and the reality of our uniqueness. I believe we all have an individual specific purpose in life, a reason for being here.

29

The human body is a work of engineering excellence. Such a work of excellence could not possibly be created and crafted for a life of mediocrity. Even today, scientists, researchers and medical professionals are still trying to figure out the complexities of the body not to mention the brain. They have made some incredible discoveries but are nowhere near to tapping the depth and breadth of untapped potential they feel exists.

I do know this: people were made for discovery, accomplishment and relationships. Many times people have tried to cage or hold back the excellence of human ingenuity and creativity. For example, the commissioner of patents in 1891 declared, "All that ever has been invented or needs to be invented has been invented." That absurd comment was made before electricity, cars and telephones were invented, not to mention computers, microwaves, cell phones and Hawaiian pizza! Imagine that? How would you like to be known for stating that little nugget of wisdom? Look before you leap, and think before you speak.

The point I make is this: we will always have the "nay-sayers" that will tell us, "Don't set your sights too high, you don't want to be disappointed!" Or, "Be happy with what you have, and don't push so hard." They'll add something profound like, "We're just concerned that you'll burn yourself out and get hurt trying to get something you may never have been meant to have or achieve." All I can say to that is "That's just negative and pessimistic thinking!" I would rather burn out shooting for excellence any day rather than settling for average, or worse, leftovers! When I look at the wonders of the human body and the unique beings that we are, I know we are not meant for average accomplishments. Always adjust your sights much higher than average. If you can dream it and see it, you can achieve it. God won't give you a dream without a way to achieve it. Don't let anyone take away your desire for excellence. Excellence is the highest standard achievable by man. Total perfection is not humanly possible, but excellence is a mark worthy of accomplishment.

To be the best of the best, la crème de la crème should be the only acceptable standard. Imagine if that was the attitude, and ultimately the legacy, passed down by every adult to future generations? We couldn't help but get better!

Fortunately, there is a fair percentage of people who continually decide to program their minds with the positives of life. They program themselves with the attitude of focusing on achieving excellence in all that they do. They associate with excellence, and they surround their lives with excellent things. They understand and they practice the law of the harvest; you reap what you sow and whatever you plant carefully and maintain will yield in return the same measure if not greater. In other words, an investment of excellence will bring a return of excellence. That's what makes the difference. Excellence is a decision! Excellence is powerful, and it's influential; once you have experienced it, you will want more.

My favorite illustration of excellence is captured in a print that is in my office. Framed in black aluminum, a mature and majestic bald eagle is in full flight with its wings outstretched and curled at the tips, poised to make another graceful and powerful downward stroke. The clouds are the only background to the piercing, focused look of determination. To me, the image is the embodiment of excellence. It includes a caption, which states:

E X C E L L E N C E

"Excellence is the result of caring more than others think is wise, risking more than others think is safe, dreaming more than others think is practical and expecting more than others think is possible."

It really comes down to programming. What are you telling yourself and what do you really want to accomplish? Look at yourself and know that you are unique. You are excellent by design, and don't let anyone tell you any different.

When people feel very sad day in and day out, it's because they have programmed themselves to be that way. They have removed all thoughts or reasons that will allow them to feel happy. It is a primary act of focus and choice. We have more power to choose our attitude and happiness than we understand. It comes from thinking, programming, deciding and then doing. The questions that we consistently ask ourselves shape the way we think and who we become. They are also a reflection of our mind-set and what we are thinking.

Doctor Patch Adams used laughter and positive attitude adjustments to actually help people get better and prolong their lives by what they were led to focus on. He would focus on bringing sunshine to hospital patients through laughter. He would also get them to ask themselves the right questions to reprogram their thinking. Zig Ziglar calls it "getting rid of the stinking thinking in your life."

The mind is a very powerful computer, and we must learn how to program and harness the power that's available to all of us. Instead of looking at the negative junk in your life and asking negative questions that compound that thinking, try looking at the things that are good or great and begin to build on those.

There's power and energy in positive questions. The mind can be programmed for positive thoughts and actions with questions that promote the positive. Be determined to ask questions until you get the right answers. Be aware of your voice tonality when asking questions. A tone can easily reflect and communicate your attitude. People will pick up on the positive energy in your voice just as they can pick up the negative. You can influence the kind of response just by the very tone of your voice when asking questions.

An uninspired and unmotivated person will ask questions like, "Why is this happening to me?" or "Why am I so unlucky?" with no real desire to have an answer to those questions. They hope and pray for a handout.

A person of vision asks questions like, "How will I do this?" or "What do I need to change to make this work?" They look for a hand up and if none appears, they do it anyway.

By asking yourself the following question, you will know if you are on track for positive influence and motivation or on-track to deflate people: **Do the questions you ask people zap them of their energy and motivation or do your questions empower and energize people by putting them on a positive thinking track?**

The questions that we ask others can and will shape them one way or another. Remember that the questions we ask ourselves reflect our thoughts, so questions can also direct other people's thoughts. We hold incredible potential to influence others with our attitude and the way we program our minds.

What are you actually telling people with the words and tone you choose in response to their inquiries? You can communicate an attitude, a personality or both. What kind of attitude, emotion or lack of emotion is in your response when people ask, "Good morning, how are you today?" Do you respond with a negative energy response, a lukewarm response or a **power** response?

The kind of response you give can speak volumes about your attitude, your disposition and your character. When you ask people how they are doing, typically you get the standard, mechanical answer that possesses little thought and/or energy. The straight reality is that the question itself, "How are you?" most of the time typically lacks any sincere desire for really wanting to know. Often both the question and the answer are very predictable and very routine. If a hint of positive energy and genuine interest is added to the regular greeting, the results can be incredibly different. The reason is that an energetic and positive greeting is the exception and not what we normally hear. Remember, you get to control the energy or temperature of the responses that you get by virtue of the tone and energy you use in your greeting. You are 50 percent of the solution to influence the response **you** want to hear.

33

If someone happens to give a **power** response in place of the regular "OK," or "I'm fine; I guess," it causes you to stop and flash them a second look. We have come to expect the same routine responses! Have an attitude adjustment, re-program your own response to an ordinary inquiry and stop someone in his or her tracks, just for fun!

(Remember the verbal programming of your computer.)

Negative energy response examples:
"I've been a lot better."   "Lousy, thank you."   "Brutal!"
"Not that great."   "Don't even ask."   "I'm beat."

Lukewarm response examples:
"Oh, not too bad."   "Okay."   "Not bad."
"I'm fine."   "I guess I'm alright."

POWER response examples:
"Tremendous."   "Just great thanks."   "Superb."
"I'm excellent."   "Fantastic."   "Dynamite."

Decide to have a positive power response of your own, and commit to responding to every greeting that way. Do that non-stop for 30 days. If you mess up and answer in a lukewarm or negative fashion, you have to start over at day one. Your power response will become a regular, habitual response and potentially become a trademark you'll be known by. Speak positive words to program your actions. Associate with positive people, and they will rub off on you! Surround yourself with "win, win" type people, and you'll become "win, win" also!

"If you think you can't, you're right and
if you think you can, you're right again."
Henry Ford

People don't like to have to think anymore, because it's too hard. We live in an instant or drive-thru society where we are not made to wait for anything. We have been programmed to expect everything right away. *Express* this and *Quick* that!

So much is readily available for us to use and make our lives easier that we have the same level of expectation for almost everything we do. We need to learn patience, and right now! More and more people are not trained or equipped to handle challenges and adversity. Welcome adversity that challenges you and makes you think. Thinking is not thought of very highly these days! Have the attitude that a setback or an obstacle is only a temporary situation, an opportunity to re-load and blast forward. I have met many a university student who can solve a math or science formula but can't solve a common sense challenge. Use your life experience and acquired skills to find alternative ways of overcoming obstacles.

If you don't have experience, make mistakes and gain experience. Roll up your sleeves and get your hands dirty or find someone that has the experience so you may glean and learn from him or her. If something works keep doing it. If something doesn't work, you now know what not to do. Regroup, adjust and keep moving. Don't be afraid to fail. The only time you don't want to fail is the last time you try!

I recall the story of a young executive during one of his first visits to the senior executive suites at head office. While he was there, he was fortunate enough to have been invited for a brief audience with the chairman of the board. The young man was always impressed with the legendary stories he had heard from his colleagues about the chairman's success and rise to the head of the company. He admired this man he had never met. He keenly wanted to understand what it was going to take for himself to one day be the leader of a big corporation.

The chairman's office was a rather large and intimidating retreat with subdued lighting and natural sunlight leaking in through partially opened blinds on several large windows. The pungent odor of cigar prevailed. He was waved to come in without a word. A large puff of smoke emptied from the side of the chairman's mouth as he leaned on the desk with both arms locked straight awaiting the junior man's approach, as he stood erect. The distinguished, gray-haired man extended his hand to greet him.

He then directed him to sit in one of the old leather armchairs that faced his gigantic glass - covered oak desk.

The young man began with an appreciative "thank you" for the audience with him and after some brief small talk the young man posed some thoughtful and calculated questions about the chairman's rise to success. Hoping for a lengthy dissertation, he asked, "Sir, what would you say was the most important thing that helped you become the chairman of the board?" He calmly but confidently gave his answer in one word, "Experience." He stated it and stared back at him with a thoughtful look and squinting eyes. To which the young executive continued. "And sir, how did you manage to accumulate such experience?" With one eyebrow raised he uttered, "Good decisions!" Leaning forward the inspired but curious young man dug deeper. "And how did you ever know how to make these good decisions?" The CEO rocked back in his leather chair and allowed the crackle of the leather to subside before he smiled and shared, "By making bad decisions! We must strive to learn from our mistakes to succeed!"

This story reminds me to see obstacles as opportunities and to grow and develop tenacity; quitting is not an option! Overcoming adversity builds your confidence and your self-esteem. It's not the size of the man in the fight, but the size of the fight in the man. So, be consistently persistent!

"Never, never, never, give up."
Sir Winston Churchill

Let's review some attitude and programming keys:

Attitude reflects actions	Program only positive
Think optimistically	Give power responses
Promote strengths of others	Read positive books
Get rid of "stinking thinking"	Welcome adversity
Don't just do, think first	Do not be afraid to fail
Ask questions that empower	Energize people positively
Associate with positive people	Quitting is not an option

36

3

FIRST IMPRESSION

Typically, the first few minutes of any relationship sets the tone and the direction the relationship will take...

Have you ever heard this? "We met, and we clicked."

First impression is all about being relatable to others. If you want to increase your overall "relate-ability," pay attention to these three areas: your personal appearance, your body language and your etiquette, both social and corporate. It takes an investment in time and effort, but the rewards are worthwhile.

The way people see you that first moment you meet is the way that they will "imprint" their memory and determine how they are going to remember you. So, as the saying goes, if you only get one chance to make a first impression, wouldn't it make sense to make the best impression possible?

Obviously the first opportunity you have to build your impression with someone is a visual one. What a person sees in your appearance, your attire, your grooming and your physical conditioning is under your control. If you value yourself, then it will show in how you dress, in your posture and how you speak about yourself and others. This reflects the level of self-esteem and the degree of pride you have. In someone's mind, if you dress shabbily, he or she will assume your work habits and your life in general is the same. Make a positive statement to someone before you even say a word. If what people see, is an impressive image of you, they will tend to show you the respect worthy of that image. Make an effort to earn that consideration by looking impressive.

The 'D' and 'C' personality types will often be noticeably sharper and more coordinated in their attire. Dressing for success and looking impressive are tasks that these people aspire to. The often bossy 'D' and organized 'C' people may both need to be a little more relaxed and welcoming with people. They need to remember clothing alone does not make the person.

Clothing can be used to create a perception or make a statement about the kind of person you are or are trying to be! Just remember that beauty is only skin deep and looks can deceive! If you dress for success, how you communicate and treat people will quickly verify the legitimacy of the visual impression you have presented.

The 'S' and 'I' personality types are more relatable to a wider range of people, because they love to be around people. The high 'I' will wear whatever is colorful, bright and available. Impression is not typically something that they get too concerned over, because people are more the focus for them. So, both 'S' and 'I' types may need to get some help and direction with the proper and appropriate attire specific to their activity. Their attitude is "As long as we're basically covered and/or comfortable, we're good to go."

Despite your personality type, you can make a good first impression if you decide that's what you want to do. If you have challenges in this area, like a high 'S' person may or even a high 'I' type personality, you may want to seek out a high 'C' person and ask for help. Keep in mind you should be prepared for the full treatment and don't question them. Even in spite of your clothing, most people will be receptive to you if you are personable and considerate toward them. Choosing to be conservative or not so radical with your clothing just increases your odds to be more relatable with people. Just because something is cool and perhaps the newest trend does not mean it's always relatable.

Be ready to greet new people properly with a firm handshake, make eye contact and build rapport. Men, do not do the clamp-grip when you shake hands, especially on a woman's hand. They often have smaller hands than men and wear rings that could potentially cause a painful greeting for them. My wife clued me in on that valuable insight. Guys, just go a little less macho. Remember that you only get one chance to make a good first impression. Make the best impression you can by attempting to connect with whoever you are speaking to.

If you want to do business or build a relationship with someone, you are the one who has to adjust and make the effort to be more relatable. It has everything to do with not focusing on yourself, but instead focusing your energy and attention on the other person.

If you carefully choose your words and comments and express them in a proper tone, it will create a climate for good communication. A person that curses every second word or always complains and criticizes may tarnish a positive visual first impression that may have been established by being well-dressed and well-groomed.

The way in which you say something will always impact someone more than what you say.

In business, your attire is a vital part of establishing a rapport of confidence and trust. For the most part, people are very visual and will generally make a judgment about you when they first set eyes on you. That judgment will be a reflection of your clothing; that's just human nature! Unfortunately we all do it, so, it will help you tremendously if you understand proper business attire as it relates to your clientele and/or audience.

That is where the expression "dress for success" came from. Success is an attitude, and it shows up in the clothing you wear! Match and choose your clothing styles and colors correctly so they are complimentary and reflect a professional image. The best choice when unsure what to wear is to be conservative. You can't lose with conservative styles. K.I.S.S. Keep it simple, and smart.

Appropriate business attire for the men would include a dark navy or black suit, white shirt and a tie with some red in it. I suggest no cartoon characters or logo ties for business. Wear polished black shoes and dark socks; save the white socks for the athletic shoes. I recommend a clean-shaven face with no earrings. Keep jewelry like chains and rings to a minimum.

Ladies might consider a similar color scheme. A knee - length skirt or pants, matching business suit jacket, with a white blouse would be appropriate. Make up that is suitable for the business environment would be best. For panty hose, the suggestion is to match the color to the skirt and finish the ensemble with the closed toe, dark shoes with moderate to low heels. Avoid tongue or any facial piercing.

For both sexes, clean and cut your fingernails. Neatly brush your hair and keep it appropriately trimmed. Brush and floss your teeth. Nothing beats a clean bright smile! A smile is an invitation to a conversation. A smile sets a warm friendly mood. Try it. Smile at someone and say, "Hi there; isn't it a great day?" You will rarely get less than a smile in return.

It takes only 17 muscles to show a smile, but it takes 41 muscles to make a frown. That seems like much more work for poorer results. If you make a living from speaking on the phone, perhaps as a telemarketer or in everyday sales, it is understood that people can feel a smile in your voice over the phone line. Are you looking for better results on the phone? Try smiling!

With a facial expression, you can demonstrate your mood, attitude or emotion before you even speak one word. Facial expressions can show disagreement or disapproval as well as acceptance and receptivity. Body language can be very telling. Picking up on body language is what I refer to as visual listening. The way we communicate non-verbally has a lot to do with our personality. I feel body language is a very important and underestimated part of communication.

Body language is an excellent indicator and a valuable tool for the effective communicator if you know how to read it and use it. If you have teenage children as I do, you will know just how real and telling this kind of communication is. Rolling eyes, looks of disbelief or the ever popular "Are you for real?" glare. Body language is something you began to use with regularity as small toddlers. Remember the pouting, the folding of your arms tightly in front of you and stamping your feet that you did this week? Well, that started a long time ago!

These are strong examples of our early body language development. As children, our parents used facial expressions and hand movements to enhance our understanding of what they were trying to communicate. This was only one of the many forms of early childhood education we received. We acquired many of our movements from observing our family members. The various types of body language that we were exposed to as kids and teenagers has been the main influence for what we are able to read and interpret as adults. It is a very important part of our everyday communication.

When you first meet people, be deliberate but discrete about observing them. Often, you can see a 'D', 'I', 'S' or 'C' personality in their movements. Look for key indicators in their actions or expressions. If you watch people closely, their out-going and energetic or reserved and focused styles will appear evident. Identifying this will help you adjust quickly to others and communicate effectively to help create the best first impression possible. We are not as observant as we should be and miss out on obvious indicators that can help us with our first encounters.

Very Important Principle: Learn to be more observant!

Staying physically fit will help you to make a good first impression. Having a regular, daily exercise routine or physical activity will help you with good posture. Being physically fit also communicates a non-verbal message to people that you care about your health and that you have some self-discipline. Your posture and your body language alone will often speak louder than words. For instance, your body language can communicate if you are happy to see someone or not. Try not to walk or stand with slouched or rounded shoulders. Stand tall with shoulders squared and your head held up. It will indicate that you are proud of who you are. If you have self-respect, I believe it will show in your posture. People will extend to you the measure of respect that you give yourself.

Your physical posture (i.e. in the way you sit or stand) can also show if you are really listening or not. If you are sitting in your seat leaning toward and looking at the person who is speaking, you will communicate that you are interested. However, if you are slouched back in a chair tapping your foot and gazing around, it will communicate very clearly that you are not.

We often make our feelings known without even meaning to communicate them. An obvious sign like arms folded across your body will usually indicate that you are upset, angry or just negative. Folded arms are never usually associated with a happy person! Try uncrossing your arms and smile!

High 'D' type personality and even high 'C' people have to be careful that they aren't so intense, serious or focused that their facial expression reflects a scowl and scares people away. They can get so focused on what they're doing or thinking that people would be prompted to ask them, "What's wrong?" or "What are you upset about?" Their answer would be "Nothing, why?" Most of the time, they don't even realize that they're looking so scary! They need to soften the expression on their face, because it often reflects the intensity of their personality and that intimidates people. This is something that these intense personalities need to pay some attention to if they want to be more influential with people.

Growing up, you picked up the way family and friends communicate through body language in everyday discussions and relationships. I encourage you to be observant and try to remember and use what you may already know. It is amazingly helpful and practical information to keep on file.

Let's review some keys to making a good 1st impression:

No clamp-grip handshakes	Smile
Remember, people are visual	Good hygiene
Match clothing styles and colors	Be observant
Wear appropriate business attire	Eye contact
Watch your posture and body language	Be physically fit

4

THE FIRST RULE OF COMMUNICATION

Listen, did you hear that?
Probably not, because you were talking too much!

I heard a speaker say this once, "God gave us two ears and one mouth. Do you suppose he is trying to tell us something?"

Principle: Listen twice as much as you speak. (First rule)

Almost anyone can talk, but it takes more skill to listen. When you are talking to people, if you want to be considered a great conversationalist, ask them questions about themselves and then just listen. Then listen some more. Use conversational bridges to keep people talking about themselves like, "Tell me more," and "Then what." Remember, the most important thing in the world to people you are talking to is them. Human nature tells us that if you're interested in me, I'll be interested in you. This is a general directive for all the personality types, because usually we are interested in ourselves first. It's a "me-first" world we live in.

To further illustrate our natural tendency towards "me-first" thinking, what happens when you see a group photograph with you in it? Who do you look for first? You, of course! This is a reality of human nature, and we must try to realize and understand our tendencies to be able to deal with them.

The 'S' type personality is a model listener because of their easygoing, supportive and people-oriented nature. They are the least talkative of all the personalities. They will do whatever they can to show you that they care. The other personalities would do well to learn from their example.

The 'I' individual loves being with people also, but typically wants to do all the talking. They will even answer their own questions for you. Unless what you've got to say is much more fun than what they have to say, they feel they can listen later. There has to be some adjusting on their part.

The '**D**' type personality as well as the '**C**' type will also be in need of some help to be more attentive because tasks and not people are their primary focus. 'D's' are too busy getting things done.

'**C's**' most of the time will allow you to talk providing you are not being silly or uninformative. They have little patience for that! They want specific details and don't want to waste their time. That bothers them tremendously.

Our dominant '**D**' person will want to know, "What's the bottom line? Cut to the chase, and let's get some work done! There may be time to talk later." 'D's' are really not too interested in listening unless it's relevant and to the point.

As previously stated, we are all driven by self-interest. One of the toughest but greatest lessons a human being can learn is this: Do what you are told! This goes against our very nature. Most, if not all of us, must be re-programmed to think differently. We must think of others first and not ourselves.

If we only talk to people about ourselves unsolicited without creating a two-way dialogue, then we will be going against the grain of most people. Adjectives such as self - centered, egocentric and mindless chatterbox come to their mind and these are labels that are hard to shed! It would be tough to build an environment for open discussion when you do all the talking. If you engage people to talk about themselves and ask questions that build on that momentum, it becomes more comfortable for them to openly share with you.

Clear indicators for "against-the-grain" communication:

Exchange the words **"I, me, my, mine"**

For one word **"You"**

Asking questions about another person, their interests, likes and dislikes, is a high form of flattery. Lean towards them and focus on what they say. Always look at the person who is talking; it shows that you are truly interested.

Early in my sales career I was having a meeting with someone who I thought was a very impressive person and who I admired very much. He was the owner/president of the company where I worked. He had accomplished great success and lived a very comfortable lifestyle because of it. So, at the end of our meeting, I asked him a question that I frequently ask people of his position: "What do you feel are the three most important skills salespeople should possess if they are to have extraordinary success?" After two or three minutes of reflective thought (it seemed much longer), he looked up at me and said, "Gord, that's a great question! I want to put some thought into my answer, because the answers are as important as the question." After a few moments of thoughtful reflection, he answered me this way:

"The number one thing you must do, above all else if you want above average success is **be a great listener.** Listen and understand what you heard, then repeat it back so you are sure you understood what was said. I believe the most important part of successful communication is listening."

"The number two thing is **become a problem-solver.** The biggest moneymakers in the world are problem-solvers. That doesn't mean just coming up with the answer, it also means finding a solution. Solve a problem for someone and provide direction with the steps to follow that will help them to move on. They will respect and admire you and never forget you."

"The number three thing is **become a friend** not just a supplier. Building a relationship with your clients will help you to build a dynasty. Relationships create referrals. Referrals are the gateway to massive success. Instead of adding, you are now multiplying growth. If people know you are genuinely concerned for their well - being they will stick with you. Loyalty in a client or friend is pure gold. These things will make you wealthy and very referable if you practice them consistently."

That was great advice that I've taken to heart and practiced.

Find people you look up to, people who have qualities you admire or skills you feel you can learn from and allow them to mentor you. Interview them and listen. Learn what they know. Take notes and grow from their knowledge and experience. Learning from the wisdom of others is priceless!

Communication is a big part of who we are and who we want people to believe we are. A good listener will always advance faster in personal relationships than a good talker.

To become a better communicator you need to be in "learning" and "growing" mode at all times. Read books and listen to CDs or cassettes that promote positive thinking and personal growth. As outlined in chapter one, we must learn to better understand people and their personality style. If we know how we are personally wired and what our basic tendencies are, we will then begin to understand others better as well. This will help us to listen more effectively.

"We learn nothing from telling. But, there is no limit to what we can learn by asking and listening."
David J. Schwartz

The average person does not do the things that will take them from the average to above-average. For massive success, you need to be willing to do more than the average person and do it more often. Be consistent with your attitude and persistent in your actions. Strive for excellence!

Let's review some keys to good communication:

2 ears, 1 mouth	Focus
You not I, me, my, mine	Ask questions
Be a great listener	Lean towards them
Become a friend	Find a mentor and learn
Become a problem-solver	Look at the person talking

5

MAKE EVERYBODY FEEL LIKE A SOMEBODY

The one thing we can all agree upon is that we all like to be recognized, especially for the good things that we do. What's that old saying? Recognition - old men die for it and babies cry for it. Very few people feel comfortable complimenting and lifting others up. Most of us fall short and need to develop some of the skills that we'll explore in this chapter. We need to remember that this is not something that comes naturally for most of us. To boost other people is a skill. It takes deliberate training and practice to become natural at it.

The high 'S' personality is the one that perhaps will have the easiest time helping someone feel like "a somebody." It is a more natural process for them than for the other personalities. They may do this out of admiration, support or just to be nice. Even if someone isn't a "nice person" or friendly, 'S's' will usually make an extra effort to give that someone the benefit of the doubt, because they really wouldn't want anyone to think badly about them.

The 'I' personality loves recognition and being at the center of all the action. However, being people-oriented, the 'I' type person will more often than not, have an easier time lifting other people up, providing they don't totally hog the spotlight.

The 'C' type would be most hesitant to lift someone up in recognition. They are always concerned about making the right choice. They compliment or encourage someone after careful scrutiny. 'C' types want to determine if they have done something perfectly. It must impress them and be worthy of their appreciation. Be careful, 'C's', not to set your expectations of people too high. That can apply pressure and alienate people.

Our dominant 'D' types may have to take their focus off the task at hand and the urgency they have placed on it in order to recognize the contributions of the people around them.

'**D**' individuals may have difficulty remembering the "people" side of the equation, because they are such doers in the "task" dimension. It has to be a deliberate move. If a '**D**' makes an effort to at least recognize or even compliment someone, that's a good start. They need to make it genuine and show some feeling. They need to try not to appear too mechanical! '**D's**' will perhaps need to make a specific effort to make this a priority if they want to become more influential, because most people often feel better just staying out of their way.

So, if we understand that making people feel "like a somebody" is not something most of us do automatically, where do we go from here? First, we must accept and agree that we are all selfish creatures, and we tend to think of ourselves first. We must be taught to consider others and not live in the "me, myself and I" world! Like listening, we must be deliberate at applying this skill of lifting people up. If we are going to get better at this, it has to become a natural part of our daily thought process. It has to be deliberate.

The nice things that we do make us feel great. If people happen to notice and acknowledge what we did and openly appreciate our contributions, this can "light our fire" in a big way! It may seem small in the eyes of worldly accomplishments but to us, it becomes significant. We would like to think that all the good things we do are very important and worthy of recognition; this is especially magnified if you are an '**I**' type personality. Recognition is one of their primary drives.

A large muffler company had a slogan that confidently stated, "We make you feel like a somebody." Their intent was to sell you a muffler, but they were also going to make you feel great in the process! It was a great marketing campaign and slogan that spanned several decades. Everyone wants to feel like they are a "somebody!" When people feel like a "nobody" (i.e. ignored and unappreciated), it generates an empty and cold feeling. In the same way, if people are unappreciated in their work environment, they will feel defeated and/or drained of their desire to perform. In contrast, if they are appreciated on the job, it can energize and empower them.

Productivity has been proven to increase dramatically when companies initiate recognition programs for good performance and a positive attitude on the job. People want to be recognized and feel like their efforts are at least acknowledged. That creates a win-win environment.

Principle: Catch people doing good and kind things and compliment them. It will make them feel important.

Don't go out of your way looking for reasons to show people where they might have gone wrong. I always encourage my kids to look for those that are doing something good or kind and recognize it by complimenting them. We ask them to share those experiences with us around our supper table in the evening. This allows them to feel good when reporting their act and reinforces looking for the good in others, not the bad.

When I took the Dale Carnegie sales course and read Carnegie's great book, *How to Win Friends and Influence People,* I learned a fundamental lesson in human behavior about how to treat people. He wrote, "Don't criticize, condemn or complain." To criticize others is generally the attempt to put others down with negative words that "de-edify" and demean. Criticizing, condemning and complaining will not lead to winning friends and influencing people!

The sweetest sound to a person is his or her name, so use it as often as you can. Include a person's name as a regular part of your conversation like, "So, Gord, what do you do for a living?" Try to look people in the eye when you speak with them. Nod in affirmation and pay close attention to what they're saying. Let the words people speak sink in **before** you respond. Wherever possible, look for ways to be in agreement with others. It's okay to disagree, just don't be disagreeable! Anybody can disagree, but it takes a wise and skilled people person to stand back and know when to be strategically silent.

**"A drop of honey catches more flies
than a gallon of gall (vinegar)."**
Abraham Lincoln

49

Honestly try to see things from the other person's point of view. That's called empathy. As a high 'D', I found it very difficult to understand, let alone practice empathy. A phrase that my very high 'S' mom used to apologetically offer me was, "Don't judge a person until you have walked a mile in their shoes." I was always very critical of others, and it took some time for me to change my thinking, but knowing is the biggest part of doing. Once I was made aware of my negative behavior, I had a choice to make. Ultimately, I wasn't able to change my results until I applied the corrective measures I had learned. I was a know-it-all 'D', so it was not easy.

Asking people for their advice, especially in areas of their strength would surely make them feel important. People love showing and telling others about the things that they do well. Highlight that! Help bring some sunshine into someone's day. If someone happens to know more about something than you, ask him or her, "You're really good at this; would you help me out?"

Compliment people as often as you can with your true feelings and thoughts. Your compliment can be the difference in an ordinary day and a great day. Catch people performing an act of kindness for someone. Specifically be on the lookout for it and compliment and praise them for their actions. We seem to have no problem pointing out people's faults or wrongdoings and nailing them. Instead, put your energy into highlighting the positive that you see and build people up. Try to "make their day." You'll leave a good impression and influence their thoughts in a good way. As much as you like to feel like a "somebody," make the effort to help others feel like a "somebody" first.

Let's review some keys to making people feel like a "somebody":

Try to be in agreement	Ask them for their advice
Look them in the eye	Show them genuine interest
Be an encourager	Give genuine compliments
Catch people doing kind things	Walk a mile in their shoes

6

INFLUENCE 101

"The key to successful leadership today is influence, not authority."   *Kenneth Blanchard*

What is influence? Webster defines it as a person's indirect power over men, events or things through wisdom, wealth and force of character (not physical) to sway authority. This is a basic definition to give us a foundational understanding of a complex word. It takes a lot of skill to exercise influence over anything or anybody. The encouragement I want to offer is that skills are not a gift you have at birth, they are all learned. If you want to become a person of influence, you can acquire the skills that are needed. Let's start with some foundational building blocks.

Main building blocks for Influence:

- Focus on the needs of others first - **Invest in People**
- Set goals and accomplish them – **Get Results**
- Be a person of your word – **Have Integrity**
- **Earn Respect** and **Admiration** with your words and actions

• **Invest in people**

We are led by self-interest. We think about ourselves more than any other topic. Just knowing that human beings have a nature of self-interest provides us with an important point of understanding to become a person of influence. This gives you power and a strategic advantage in dealing with others. Many of the things that are outlined in this chapter and throughout this entire book sprout from this basic understanding. Focus on someone other than yourself, and you're already going to be ahead of the game. Looking out for # 1 is part of human nature. If you put your focus on others; however, you now cater to their core interest – them! That appeals to them, and they'll like that.

- **Invest in people** (continued)

We all desire to accomplish and acquire different things in our lives, our careers and in our relationships. We should never assume that others want what we want or like what we like. In the process of maturing as a person, we hopefully will learn that the universe does not revolve around us. In addition, the more we make the specific effort to focus on others, the more we will actually gain influence and favor with people. The following principle will help you more than any other thing you do if you take ownership of it and practice it.

Principle: "You can have everything out of life that you want if you will just help enough other people get what they want out of life. " *Zig Ziglar*

Excellent words to live by! I am a very high 'D' with a secondary high 'I' personality. My internal motor activity is outgoing with a primary orientation that is task-driven but is also followed closely by a people-driven style. In others words, I like to be with people as long as I am in charge. They better do what I say, and they better have fun doing it! So as you can see, the Ziglar quote did not strike a responsive chord in me. Let's just say that I'm a work-in-process when it comes to changing my thinking and the way I look at people and circumstances.

I have found in my life and throughout my career, that when I put my focus on the benefit and well - being of others, my life takes on a totally different direction with special meaning. The drive to do things for others has a different energy to it, than doing something just for myself. This kind of focus requires that you ask specific questions of those you want to help and listen carefully to their responses. Determine what it is they want and when they want it. Then set some goals, establish a plan and then work together to help them achieve it. That is what you call "making an investment" in people, and it's the only kind of investment that will usually bring a positive return.

• **Invest in people** (continued)

If you can help people accomplish their goals and dreams, you will have their admiration and friendship for life. This adds tremendous value to life and living. Influence growth and influence progress with a targeted purpose.

The personality that would have the easiest time and be most comfortable with making this investment would be a person with a primary 'S' or potentially an 'I' type personality because of the dominant people side of their orientation. The 'S' type would prefer to see you accomplish all you could, even before them because of their supportive and easygoing nature. They want to influence you with intangibles like encouragement, respect and admiration. These are held in high regard for a high 'S' individual.

High 'I' people would certainly make a valiant effort at investing in you to help you get what you want, especially if their secondary style was 'S' *and* it meant they would be guaranteed some good fun in the process. Nevertheless, they would have to maintain focus on your particular goals to get results.

Our 'C' type people would rather recommend or point out the specific steps you would need to follow to get what you want, and if they had a 'D' secondary style, they would be happy to show you the way also! As a 'C' with a blend of 'S', if you could list your specific goals and show the detailed step - by - step plan you have established to help you get what you want, they would certainly approve of your idea if they were certain you could carry it through to its completion.

Most people don't really set any kind of goals at all, short - term or long - term, unless they're an "achieving" high 'D' or a "have a plan" high 'C' or a combination of those two traits.

High 'D' people will invest in you if you are a serious doer and a no-nonsense type. They don't like to waste time and lose any momentum in the process. Really, they would rather not get involved with you, but if they did, they would get results!

- **Invest in people** (continued)

A high '**C**' with a '**D**' personality blend can tend to be a bossy and organized person who generally prefers to make things happen without people around. Goal - setting and accomplishment in an organized fashion is what this combination is all about, but they need to remember people!

Realize this, no matter what personality you are, if you focus on the needs of others first, you will have always made the wisest investment. Investing in other people will often be inconvenient and not always your first or favorite choice, but the return feeling of satisfaction knowing that you did the right thing is everything! You will have given of yourself.

- **Get Results**

Certainly, the average person may have an idea of what he or she would like to have or like to accomplish some day; however, a goal will usually never be fully realized if it's not written down with a date set upon it.

Mere thoughts and desires would qualify as a fantasy. You will never hit a target if you cannot actually see that target. Specific goals are essential for consistent and focused success. The goals you set for yourself will influence a positive outcome even if you don't hit them. I encourage you to have something that you can look to as a marker that will give you incentive. **See it**! I'm sure you have heard the stories about exhausted athletes who failed to finish a race, because they couldn't fix their eyes on the finish line beyond a hill only meters away. Set your sites on a goal that you can visually fix your eyes to focus on and drive toward.

The high '**D**' personality has no problem getting results. Others better stay out of the way, because if the bottom line is achieving results, that's the gas that powers their motor. They may need to be less determined and more cautious and careful not to create too many casualties in the process of getting things done. They need to look to get things accomplished with people rather than doing it for people.

• **Get Results**   (continued)

High 'C' people think their way through to get results with a well-devised plan. It will take logical, consistent action and minimal effort. Stay out of their way, and don't mess with their plans! Completing the task on time and keeping up appearances is all that matters.

High 'I' individuals have a focus challenge, and it will be the one thing they will have to overcome to get any results, let alone consistent results. Just to initiate thinking about a goal is a victory. 'I's' must start with very short-term goals and score some victories there and build some history of achievement.

Our sweet 'S' person has to be less indifferent and start to care about getting specific results. An 'S' has to first decide to make a decision – any decision. "Yes, I will do that," instead of "Oh, it doesn't matter. Whatever you want to do is fine." Any goals and results are okay with 'S's'. As long as you're happy, they're happy. 'I' and 'S' types can drive the 'C' and 'D' types crazy very quickly!

Whatever your tendency, you must have a plan of action prepared in advance that will allow you to accomplish your goal. Be patient, but remain alert and ready for an opportunity to presents itself. When it does, apply the plan and move toward your goal. Remember to be observant so you don't miss it.

Plans and goals are different. The goal is the destination. The plan represents the steps you will take to arrive at the goal. If an obstacle or setback appears, the goal should never change; the plan (steps) just needs to be altered. Change your action plan to get to your goal and remain focused. Don't quit and head for home. Leaders persevere!

Those who get results are influential; they inspire people. Those who are organized are influential; people follow them. Those who have a strong work ethic are influential; people admire them. Those who are effective communicators are influential; they motivate people.

• Get Results (continued)

Those who set goals and accomplish them are influential; they have credibility. Those that put others ahead of themselves are influential; they win people's loyalty and respect. Influence is a valuable and prized possession.

Winners focus on the solutions, not on the problems.

If we perform with excellence, we will have influence to lead others. People are attracted to those who excel in their chosen endeavor. Success attracts people like a magnet. It inspires and empowers. The standard of excellence is a very high standard and something we should all strive for. So few people shoot for excellence that when someone shows up with that standard, they are very noticeable. People who have excellent standards raise the bar and not everyone will like that, but the tide raises all boats! You may ruffle some feathers, but don't be intimidated or pressured into lowering your standards. Higher standards achieve higher results, because the aim is different. A person that has influence will sometimes lead and not even know it. People may follow your example and you may not even realize it. Leaders will be people who influence others by virtue of their skills and accomplishments. The greater the impact that you want to make in the world, the greater your influence needs to be. Your job may be to teach grade four, fasten screws on a production line or direct a symphony orchestra; no matter what it is, do what you are called to do with a high standard of excellence!

• Have Integrity

"What you do, speaks so loudly that I can't hear what you are saying!" This is an expression that speaks a very clear message to me. Actions will be fueled by dominant thoughts. What you do consistently will generally reflect your mind's focus.

• **Have Integrity**   (continued)

When I was younger, I was at a pre-season tryout for hockey. The head coach told all the players before the start of the workouts, "I will hear the tongue in your mouth tell me of your intentions, but I will watch the tongue in your shoes and skates to show me the truth of your words." I never forgot that. On the same subject, a good friend who I coached university hockey with used to tell the players, "Don't give me lip service!" To elaborate: Don't tell us what you're going to do if you're not prepared to back it up with your actions. Your word is your worth! Mean what you say, and say what you mean. That's the essence of integrity. People should be able to count on you and rely on you when you tell them something that you're going to do. Your actions should be a reflection of the words you speak. Be true to your word.

The serious, high 'C' personality type will usually be more honest and forthright, because they are into accuracy, correctness and perfection. If honesty is the best policy and being truthful and honest is the acceptable standard, they will adhere to that, because it is the right thing to do.

High 'S' individuals are very trustworthy, so they can usually be counted on as people of high integrity. They may sometimes be so concerned about pleasing others that they may get suckered into saying or doing the wrong thing. Much depends upon the secondary personality blend of this person, because that will determine their ability to stand up for their beliefs.

High 'I' people will be seen as energetic allies that help others accomplish many things, but their persuasive and optimistic drive can cause them to be manipulative and unrealistic; therefore, harder to believe all the time. They need to keep things under control when they're talking and not exaggerate the facts to make things sound more attractive than they really are.

57

• **Have Integrity** (continued)

People want to believe the 'I' person so 'I's' need to keep what they say believable, rather than "to good to be true."

'D' individuals carry a double-edged sword! They can be easy to trust, because they appear to be so confident and natural as leaders. Most people, especially 'S's' and 'I's', will often not even question a 'D's' choice, because 'D's' seem so in control. On the other hand, they can be hard to trust, because of the often intense and serious approach they have to life. 'D's' have a tendency to be very self-reliant and this will cause others to feel that they are not needed and thus alienated. 'D's' prefer to do things on their own. If their competitive and results-oriented drive doesn't become too pushy or dictatorial, people will look to them for direction and answers. If 'D's' become less abrasive and offensive, it will increase their chances of being trusted.

• **Earn Respect and Admiration**

Never tell people outright that they are wrong! When people are wrong or do something wrong, they may admit it to themselves, but they will come to defend their decision quite strongly should someone tell them that very same fact. This statement is amplified if people sense that it is said to potentially embarrass them. Ridicule, negative slurs and abusive language will never win people to your side.

Socrates, the great Greek philosopher, was credited with being one of the wisest persuaders in the world. He managed this with a communication technique that has become known in modern times as the "Socratic method." He was a skilled and influential communicator. He was known as one of the most learned and wise men of his time. He was always very careful not to tell people outright that they were wrong. Remember that you cannot bring people to your side if you argue and antagonize them by attacking their ideas and thoughts. You must use the skill of persuasion and ask the right questions.

• **Earn Respect and Admiration** (continued)

When Socrates was not of the same mind-set of a particular person but knew his thoughts were correct, the main focus of his discussion with that person was based on getting, "Yes, yes," responses.

Socrates would ask questions of his adversaries with which they would have to agree. He would keep on winning one admission upon another until he had nothing but a collection of yes answers! He would skillfully continue asking questions until his counterparts found themselves welcoming and embracing his conclusion. This is a skill that takes practice to be a fluid and natural part of your regular communication and selling style. Socrates would have not considered himself to be a "salesman" by profession but certainly had people "buying" into his beliefs and values based on his ability to communicate with his influential style.

Principle: Get others saying, "Yes, yes," as soon as possible.

Try not to argue with those who disagree with you if it is at all possible. 'D' individuals with their dominant, take-charge personality, and the 'C' types with their need for correctness and accuracy, will be the most challenged with this, and they will have a strong urge to disagree. While their traits can be strengths worthy of respect and admiration, their traits can also become an anchor that holds them back. When a person disagrees with them, it takes away their dominance and control and that's their security. They will need to work on this area if they want to grow in their personal influence.

Sometimes to keep the peace, we do have to agree to disagree. The 'I' and 'S' type people will naturally gravitate to being more agreeable because of their people orientation. The 'S' will seek out harmony first, and the 'I' person will seek to keep things upbeat and positive. Two favorite peace-making comments would be, "Whatever you want," or "No problem."

• **Earn Respect and Admiration** (continued)

Whenever you can, be diplomatic and create a climate for positive, low-level, open discussion. Unfortunately, folks love to "catch" other people doing things wrong. If you recognize that you're wrong about something, acknowledge it and confess it quickly! If you know for sure that you're going to get rebuked, it is better to beat another person to it and confess it openly yourself. You'll be pleasantly surprised how it will diffuse the potentially emotional outburst you may have encountered had you just taken your chances with your wrong-doing being uncovered. A gracious and forgiving attitude is the general response to a quick and truthful confession, and you will be more respected and admired for your maturity and honesty.

It is much easier to critique yourself than to hear a critique from others. Respect and admiration are major building blocks in the foundation to become a person of influence.

On the other side of the coin, should you happen to be right about something and know it, then be gracious and try to win or influence people gently and tactfully to your way of thinking. I would highly recommend not saying things like, "I told you so," and "I knew it all along!" These words will influence division between us rather than bring us together.

Sincere compliments win people's admiration, and respect will gain mutual respect.

Let's review some keys to build Influence:

Help people get the results they want	Invest in people
Help people set goals and plan steps	Get results
Get people saying, "Yes, yes"	Have integrity
Never tell people they're wrong	Earn respect
Set a standard of excellence	Earn admiration
Mean what you say	No "lip service"
Confess your mistakes	Be tactful

7

SELLING - A LIFE SKILL

I have often heard these comments from people, "I am not a salesperson!" and "I hate selling!" I will tell you one fact that I know is true and irrefutable. Everyone sells, all the time! Every day you sell yourself more than you probably realize. You cannot make it in this world if you do not sell in some way, shape or form. **Selling is life, and life is selling!**

It's interesting that there are people who are totally convinced that they do not have even one ounce of sales ability in them. So much so, that they will passionately defend their belief and spend the next few minutes telling me why they are no good at sales. I love to look at them with a smile and say, "You've convinced me. I'm sold on the fact that you are not any good at selling! Thanks for proving my point!"

Think about it for a moment. If you have ever dated or if you are married, you have sold at least once and in some cases, more than once. On your first date, you shared all of the wonderful things about yourself that would hopefully appeal to that other person. You were selling yourself hoping that your date was an interested, or at least a sympathetic "buyer." In fact, you may be better at selling than you think. Let's ask your partner or spouse. Maybe you oversold them. Are you still trying to deliver on some of those early sales promises?

To clarify this, if you have ever been hired to work for someone, you should understand that you actually "sold" him or her into hiring you. You certainly didn't tell that person about all of your deficiencies and bad habits. You sold that person on your ability to do the job better than anybody else. You where hired based on your own natural or learned ability to communicate or sell the value of you. You say, "Well, that's different!" I'm telling you it's not different at all. Like I said earlier, selling is life; life is selling.

It doesn't matter what your personality type or blend is. Each personality has the ability to sell in a unique way.

The degree to which you are convicted of your thoughts, beliefs and passion in something, is the degree to which you will be able to "sell" someone on them. If you have little to no belief or passion in your ideas or thoughts, there is usually no sale.

Toddlers, kids, teens and adults, along with their specific 'D', 'I', 'S' and 'C' connected traits are selling all the time. Selling effectively has everything to do with winning or persuading people to your way of thinking. We have all been doing this to one degree or another every single day since we were born. The key words to grasp are winning and persuading. The personality you possess will help determine the kind of approach you may have to make to get "the sale."

The high 'D' personality type will be a confident communicator, winning most people with their determination and drive. People can often feel the aura of accomplishment that emanates from the high 'D'. The 'D' person may often be so confident, they may unknowingly become forceful in their drive to accomplish their goals. People may follow a 'D' out of fear or intimidation and because of that, a 'D' type person may not always get the desired results that they had been anticipating. This frustrates 'D's', because they thrive on accomplishment and expect to be the best! Less than best to them is losing.

Our friendly 'I' people with their persuasive and optimistic words will lead people into activities with the expectation of action, fun and adventure. They are the most comfortable sellers of all the personalities, because they love to talk and nothing is ever a problem. You'll often hear them say, "No problem," and for them it's true; nothing is taken too seriously.

The high 'I' style is also prone to exaggerate and make some things sound better than they actually are. There may be some disappointments down the road for those who buy into their schemes. If the 'I's' aren't careful to set a realistic expectation of what lies ahead, they will have few followers. Fool me once, shame on you; fool me twice, shame on me.

High 'S' individuals have no problem with people and would never consider offending or taking advantage of anyone. They like people, and they are comfortable around them but prefer meeting and greeting them in a quiet and unassuming way. They do not enjoy rejection or confrontation. Typically, in any social setting, they will do much of the listening and will have people liking them quickly. High 'S' people can be such good listeners that they become uncommunicative about how they feel. They have to be careful not to be so shy that they don't share their true thoughts or feelings and miss out on some of the fun in life.

High 'C's' are typically people of very few words, but given an opportunity to share their views on how things are done, they will give you the facts and just the facts. If they are not certain, they would not say anything. There is no speculation or guessing with a 'C' type person. It's not in their nature. They can appear to be cold or distant and a challenge to befriend, because they are careful, calculated and analytical. They don't just jump right into anything, including friendships. Once they permit you to get to know them, they are very accommodating and compliant.

No matter what style or manner of communicating people adopt, they should never try to force or manipulate people to do something they don't want to do. An expression that has given me great insight into how I should communicate with people is this: *a man convinced against his will, is of the same opinion still*. This is true! It is self-explanatory and provides us with a simple but important truth about human nature; people want to make their own choices and feel good about it. Often, people will decide to go along with some things even though they are not completely comfortable with them. If they go along with a plan just to cooperate or keep the peace but their heart is not in the decision, they will not finish strong, if they even finish at all.

Don't follow anyone who's not going anywhere.

There's a great little story that proves this theory. An eight-year-old girl was in a grocery store with her mother. Her mom had asked her nicely to go and wait in the chair by the exit door while she gathered the bags into the cart. The little girl refused by saying, "Why? I don't want to!" The mother gave a stern look and a firm reply, "There are too many people and too many grocery carts here, and you may get hurt. Now, please go and sit in the chair by the door like I asked you!" The little girl crossed her arms in front of her and started walking towards the chair, when she stopped, turned and said to her mom, "Okay, I'm going to go and sit down, but in my mind I'm staying right here!"

Remember we are driven by self-interest. It is our natural tendency to ask, "Why?" This is especially true if we are asked to do something that is against our idea or plan. The young girl was convinced against her will to do something she didn't want to do. To be in the middle of the action was where she wanted to be and there was an obvious discipline or consequence attached if she continued to be disobedient. She wanted her mom to know that her act of compliance was under protest.

Most people don't like being told what to do. Depending on our personality, we may not always say, "That's not what I want to do," but our actions may speak very loudly regarding those very same thoughts. Parents will have control over their kids only for a certain length of time. Even when kids are ready to establish more independence as teens, they will still need some parental direction. They will have to be more "sold" to your way of thinking than told. Answers like, "Because I said so," will not work on teenage kids or young adults. Your ability to "sell" to your teens will depend greatly in your ability to connect and communicate in open and nonthreatening tones.

Because people do not like to be directed or told what to do, we must learn to use words that will allow people to recognize the value of your directives and suggestions, so they are able to make an informed decision. People like to feel that they made a final decision based on their own evaluation of the information available.

Skills in persuasive and influential communication are important to learn so as to allow you to engage and win people to your way of thinking.

To complement the earlier expression regarding convincing a person against their will, I offer you this quote:

**"You cannot teach a man anything.
You can only help him to find it within himself."**
Galileo

If the claim I make is true (that we all sell, all the time), it would make sense for us to be regularly developing and improving our ability to connect with and influence people. By polishing our people skills, we grow in our understanding and relate to others better. We ultimately become more effective at selling ourselves and expanding the reach of our influence.

I have experienced the most growth in my personal development when I was ready to acknowledge that I didn't know everything and that I had a specific challenge that was keeping me from advancing. I would find someone who could coach me and help me find a way to adjust and then allow me to be accountable to that person for the progress that was needed.

As long as it is up to you, and it is, try hard to be wiser and better than other people are content to be. I encourage you to never stop growing and cultivating your skill and ability to sell who you are to others. Selling is life, and life is selling!

Let's review some keys to the life skill of selling:

Believe in your natural skill and ability
Don't manipulate for your own gain
Try not to tell people what to do
Do not be driven by self-interest
Win people to your way of thinking
Learn and develop additional people skills

65

"Some men succeed because they are destined to,
But most men succeed because they are determined to."

Author unknown

8

SELLING - AS A PROFESSION

A very large part of selling as a profession is selling what you already know how to sell naturally – you. Success and longevity in professional sales relies heavily on a person's ability to establish a rapport and then build a relationship. Sounds a lot like life, doesn't it?

Realize that 90 percent of the effort in sales has to do with getting the prospect to first of all like you, or at least respect you. If people can relate to you, then they will begin to feel like they can trust you. This is all before they ever look at product or service. This is why you have to be comfortable and competent about asking personal questions and listening and being very observant. These steps can happen in a matter of minutes, and you will know and actually feel when you have accomplished this rapport with someone. If someone does not like you for some reason, or cannot relate to you, there will be no foundation to build any trust on, and there will be no sale.

Ultimately, people still want to know, "What's in it for me?" That goes for life and for business; it's no different. People don't mind if you make something in a deal, but their own needs must be adequately taken care of in the process.

Some of the most effective and successful salespeople I have met have been business owners who sell as a natural part of promoting their business. They are very diligent but also very comfortable and confident in connecting with their clientele. The high 'D' and high 'I' types with various different secondary blends seem to be most comfortable in the professional sales or business ownership environment. Nevertheless, I have met many high 'S' and 'C' people who run very successful businesses as well. Often, they strategically place a powerful high 'D' or an inspiring high 'I' in key leadership roles, like management and sales, to fuel the fires of their regular ranks. Knowing the strengths of your people and not being afraid to utilize them for the greater success of the team is key. That's being a good people person and also understanding your own limitations.

Professional selling is really a performing art. To observe accomplished sales professionals during a presentation, and to watch them probe, relate and maneuver to close the sale is a thing of beauty. There is a sense of conviction, and they talk and act like an owner. They typically will employ a feature, benefit and value pattern in their sales presentation.

You will see this confident style of selling if the owner/ president or partner of a company is the one doing the selling. Why? Because there's something different about a person who is selling his own image and product. It's called ownership. If regular salespeople can be given a sense of "ownership" or if they will adopt it as an attitude themselves, the results can be tremendously different. If you assume ownership for something, it holds greater value, and you will always work harder to keep what is yours. Your attitude and approach to selling becomes very different. That's the law of taking ownership. Owners are committed to succeed because the investment is greater; there's more to lose!

When employed as a professional salesperson to represent someone's product, I would adopt an attitude that the product or service I was selling was really mine. I found I worked harder to earn the sale with this kind of attitude.

I was always very well prepared for my customers. I knew all the important features, benefits and values of my product and the specific things that separated me from my competition. My goal was to first establish a rapport and build a relationship. Second, I would probe to find what the client was specifically looking for and identify their needs. If my product could provide the solution, I would demonstrate the appropriate feature, benefit and value to them that would meet their specific need and then I would provide them with assurances of product performance and satisfaction (i.e.: feature, benefit and value).

My approach to selling is to always take personal pride in the sales that I am representing. Then, my attitude is that I want to sell products with an "ownership" mentality. That is, as if it is my own company that I want to promote and sell.

In the corporate world of sales, there is much more emphasis and focus on professional representation and training of the feature, benefit, value selling technique. If you learn and apply this technique regularly, it will consistently raise your performance and results above that of your peers in the jungle of professional sales. **Buyers Buy Benefits!**

If you do not have an employer who is providing you with training, you may want to think about increasing your personal skill set on your own. You are not born with skills; you must learn them. To increase your skills, do not underestimate the value of investing in yourself with seminars, books, CDs /tapes and proper peer association to keep you fired up. Remember, motivation is temporary! We have to keep regenerating ourselves mentally to remain motivated and energized.

I heard something as a rookie salesperson that caused a light to go on for me, and I began to turn my activity into results. I was always busy, but I wasn't as productive as I would have liked. I heard that results and revenue in sales is totally predictable if you know your numbers. The numbers I am referring to are, how many people you must speak to in order to close a sale. Everyone's number is different, 1 person out of 3, 1 out of 10, or 1 out of 50 for example. Whatever the ratio may be, becomes your formula for predictable success. It doesn't matter if your number is high or low, your results are predictable once you know your ratio. The higher the number, the more work you obviously have to do.

Reducing your own personal number gap or ratio is based on getting consistently good at four things. These are understood as being the necessary, basic practices for being successful in sales. They are:

1. The number of people you consistently sell in front of.
2. Your ability to probe and find the true needs of your client.
3. Presenting the features, benefits and values of your product or service as they pertain to your clients' specific needs.
4. Specifically **asking** for the order.

69

Selling to get results is not only about feature, benefit and value. There are also the technical components that fit into a master plan for professional selling. These four basic stages in the sales process need to be followed to achieve consistent, high-level success. They will incorporate all of the four basic practices that were listed on page 69.

Four stages of selling: 1.   Breaking the ice
                                2.   Finding the need
                                3.   Filling the need
                                4.   Closing the sale

The preceding are important, connecting links in the chain of the sales process. For long-term, consistent results, this process will be a good practical guideline for you to follow.

Stage 1: BREAKING THE ICE

At the very beginning of any first meeting between two people, there is a period where we get to know each other or break the ice. This is the time to try to build a rapport and make a connection. The best way to find a connection with people is to talk about their favorite topic, themselves!

There is a formula that I was taught at the very start of my selling career that is excellent for initiating conversations. It was presented to me in the form of the acronym **F.O.R.M.** Each letter stands for a specific topic of conversation. These are **F**amily, **O**ccupation, **R**ecreation, and **M**otivator. This acronym provides an easy way to remember what kind of questions one could ask to get to know someone better without sounding like you were interviewing him or her for a job.

Make inquiries that will allow you to get to know that person on a more personal level. In an office, look for something that's personally connected to them like a picture, vehicle or trophy. The success or growth of their company is always a popular topic. Breaking the ice has very little to do with actual selling. It has everything to do with finding some common ground to stand on to help you to connect with your prospect.

Stage 1: BREAKING THE ICE (continued)

A spouse's or a child's photo will provide an opportunity to connect with people on family - related topics. A framed university degree will bridge a conversation into their academic history. Discover what motivates and drives them in their career and why do they do what they do? Allow them to share as openly as they would like. Many important personal details will be revealed and shared. These topics will assist you to find relatable connections so you can develop a relationship through those common ties. You can build rapport through your casual, personal conversations, and this will eventually flow comfortably into business - related discussions.

For most people, casual and personal conversations are often not easy to start. Many people that you approach have barriers they erect as a protection like invisible, protective layers or zones around them. Your ability to penetrate these zones depends on your collective personalities and your accumulated and developed people skills. For example, if a 'C' or 'D' type personality, who by nature are both less personable, have met people that have taken advantage of them before, they would be much more cautious and skeptical about any future relationships. They would keep people at arm's length for their own protection. The 'I' and 'S' personalities being more people-oriented, would be quicker to let down their guard and trust new relationships. Much depends on the blend of their secondary personality and how you connect with them. This will help determine how receptive they may be to you.

Naturally, the **F.O.R.M.** method comes easily to the already people-orientation high 'I' and high 'S' type individuals. Their conversations touch on all kinds of topics, not just business, because they want to get to know the person. The task-driven 'D' and 'C' types would be wise to implement this method. **F.O.R.M.** would help them connect with people and intentionally delay them from getting right to business. Regardless of personality, if we can learn to reference **F.O.R.M.** regularly, it can have positive effects on developing strong and profitable long-term relationships.

Stage 1: BREAKING THE ICE (continued)

In a business relationship if you are able to establish some kind of personal connection with your client, then you must remember to maintain a professional attitude. Try not to become too familiar and do things like "high-five" them when you greet them. You should respect their position and not compromise the business connection and their position.

Be careful not to blast into a person's space too fast or become too familiar, too quickly. It usually takes time to build rapport, especially in business. The more you understand this and the better you become at reading people and their reactions, the easier it will be for you. Trust must be earned.

Stage 2: FINDING THE NEED

Just as helping others get what they are looking for is the foundation for building relationships in life, finding the need that clients may have is key to being successful in the sales profession. Too many salespeople are so busy making their pitch that they don't even know exactly what the prospect needs and why!

Finding the need is not just asking, "What can I help you with today?" Not everyone will just volunteer that information freely. The questions you ask to find the need should be part of a casual conversation that will promote a comfortable level of open dialogue. Knowing the tendencies of certain personalities can become helpful in gauging your approach and also your responses to people.

If you are inquiring on a specific needs assessment, be prepared to record key answers or details that are given by prospects and clients. It shows them that you are interested and that their response is important to you. It also demonstrates to them that you are organized and responsible. This is a great way to build confidence with corporate people.

Stage 2: FINDING THE NEED (continued)

Out of courtesy, be sure to ask your clients or prospects if they mind you taking notes. Keep notes simple and concise, focusing on key details that are important. You don't want to lose valuable eye contact for too long. Note taking is an excellent practice and highly recommended to ensure that you remember important points from your meetings. Remember to refer back to them later when you prepare for your presentation and closing call. On the other hand, note taking is not the preferred way to build relationships in a social setting, so you may want to keep your note pad in your pocket for those occasions.

Not all people will be ready and willing to share what they know. All but the high 'I' types of course! If given the opportunity, they will often give you more information than you really need. Try to keep your questions for the high 'I' direct and specific, nothing that allows for a long response. The high 'D' personality if you recall, believe they don't really need help from anyone! They are so self-reliant they may find any question suggesting they need help to be almost offensive. In any case, with the 'D' be sure to get straight to the point.

The shy, high 'S' person would probably decline any offer for assistance. They would be happy with some information to study and decide later. The high 'C' personality would likely appreciate and accept your inquiries or offers for assistance. It would be more efficient and logical to solicit help and find exactly what they would be looking for. They don't want to waste valuable time! Don't get too personal though; they will want to keep it all strictly business.

The finding-the-need stage is a foundational, brick by brick building process, like an investigator finding clues to solve a crime or pieces to a puzzle. It gives you a solid, confident direction with specifics to focus on. If you can determine all of the specific needs and know that you can fill those needs with the features and benefits of your product, then you should have a high level of confidence in winning the order.

Stage 2: FINDING THE NEED (continued)

You must work systematically and tactfully to uncover the needs, because often, prospective clients will not just hand that information over. As part of finding the need with new prospects, ask what the specific criteria may be for selecting a supplier for their company as well as the product they seek. If you know what their expectations are, you will know right away if you are a serious contender. You don't want to waste your time or theirs. For existing clients, ask them what their expectations are for the order they are giving you. Never be complacent or overconfident because of familiarity.

Ask specifically about what kind of budget they have for their purchase. They may not always be willing to answer that, but if they do tell you, you will now have great ammunition to use in your closing presentation. If price is the only issue to the clients that you deal with, it's because they probably don't understand or know the value side of products. Always discuss the value connected to the price of your product, because if people understand what the true value is to them, they will be able to justify paying more for their purchase. A Mercedes Benz is a better value than a Cadillac. Why? Mercedes uses more expensive parts to build their cars, and because of that, they last longer, drive better, are much safer and have a higher re-sale. All are 'value added' benefits to the car owner.

If people tell you that they want the best price and the best value, you know that they don't really understand the higher price for value connection. Value added, costs money! If you sell value and can justify your sell price, there is always more profit available to you. If you sell only based on best price, there is usually less profit! Give clients the choice, but always try to sell value over price. If price is the only criteria for them, you know what it will take for you to get the order.

Quickly separate the browsers or "tire-kickers" from the real buyers. Ask very specific questions that will help you identify their level of commitment to buy today or sometime later.

Stage 2: FINDING THE NEED (continued)

Remember: There is power in the question. Some questions you may ask to identify a serious buyer are, "If you were to find the options you like, when would you like to take delivery?" or, "If you were to find the right program, when did you want to get started?" The responses to these kinds of questions immediately identify the serious buyers from the shoppers. Try to find their reason to buy now. Shoppers are always eventual buyers, but the buyers are the immediate focus of the sales call.

Real buyers have a sense of urgency. They have usually already decided what they want. You must methodically and skillfully uncover what their want is and then direct them to the benefits your product or service will provide. If you can manage to identify the serious buyers, you will save time. As a professional, your time is very valuable. Results are what you're after. **Results!**

You will always get better results if you plant your seeds in fertile soil. Selling as a profession is a numbers game. The more seeds you plant, the greater the harvest. If you determine prospects are serious buyers but not right now, be diligent to take good notes of the details and begin to follow up with them one month before they say they will be ready.

Once you understand what the clients' needs are and have all the information you feel is necessary to design and make your presentation, you must set the tone for your closing call. Ask them when they will be making the decision on this particular order and find out how many suppliers you are competing against. It is imperative to be the last person in for these final stages. Set an appointment for the end of the day that they would like to place the order. Be the last supplier to see them. You should also be asking a qualifying question to determine the buyer's serious consideration for your involvement. Questions like this are effective: "If we are able to meet all of the needs you have shared with me today, and our price is competitive, will we be given consideration for this order?"

Stage 2: FINDING THE NEED (continued)

This type of question is asked to set the tone and start the process of the client giving you consideration over someone else. If a client answers *yes*, this gets the prospect mentally prepared to give you the opportunity to be a serious candidate to earn his or her business. A positive response becomes more ammunition for your closing call. This is how you begin to set and direct a buyer's expectation and build some obligation. You have both made an investment of time and effort in each other and that's worth something. Be intelligent and strategic with your questions so that you can strengthen your position for the closing call.

Any answer other than yes should throw up a red flag. You may have missed something in uncovering the prospect's needs, or you could be just wasting your time. Ask why you're not a contender, and he or she will usually tell you. It is better to find out what your position is before you invest any of your time doing the preparation work to earn business you never had a chance to get.

Stage 3: FILLING THE NEED

In this stage, the professional salesperson needs to take all the accumulated information and put it all together in a clear and effective presentation. Try to always come back to the clients with some ideas to solve the challenges or fill the needs that you uncovered and discussed together. Address the way you propose to solve their challenges with your product or service. In addition to solving their challenges, you should always try to present some new and beneficial ideas that will distance you and your product from your competitors.

If you choose to only match their existing product or service and go head to head with the incumbent supplier, you stand a good chance of losing that battle. People will typically not change just for the sake of change. They will change if that change provides a benefit and a value to them. Always give them a good, logical reason to justify the change.

Stage 3: FILLING THE NEED (continued)

There is a definite strategy to approaching this meeting for consistent, successful results. In a competitive environment with one or more suppliers, the strategy is to contact clients and inquire if they have all the other supplier proposals in their possession. If they do, then set up your appointment to see them. You inform them that you have some great ideas for them to consider, and look forward to presenting them. This builds their interest and keeps them from going with any of the other options that may have already been presented. Being last to present is a very important part of your plan. If you are not the last one, you must find a way to delay your appointment. The reason for being last to present is so that you know that they now have all the other information they will need, other than yours, to make a decision. It gives you an element of control and a strategy for your closing call.

If you happen to not be in a competitive situation and you're the sole supplier, being last is not an issue. I would encourage supplying prospects or clients with two possible product or service options and sell against yourself. Give them a choice.

Once you have positioned yourself as the final presenter, your primary objective is to establish that you are still a serious contender should you meet all the criteria. After the standard pre-business conversation has concluded, you then move to qualify the person. You have to gain control of the direction that you want the meeting to go in by asking the right questions. Put the odds in your favor by having a well thought out and strategic plan to secure their business. This should help you to know where the momentum of the call is going.

As often as I can, I try to question using the Socratic method of "yes-yes" (Chapter 6) in my own way. I have become accustomed to using a powerful two-letter word that has allowed me to achieve positive results. My power word is "IF."
I always say...

...When you know the answers, the questions are easy!

Stage 3: FILLING THE NEED   (continued)

The word "IF" is the most powerful word in a professional sales-person's vocabulary. You can almost always direct a person to move in your direction with this powerful little word. You'll have their attention every time you structure your question beginning with the word "IF." It implies that there is something of value in this for them.

The key to effective benefit questions is to never present a feature-benefit statement without asking a connecting "IF" question immediately after. For example: "This particular feature allows one person to do the work of two people in the same amount of time. So, IF we can help you produce twice the amount of product with less man hours, wouldn't that have a positive impact on your profitability?" The answer is obviously, yes! We're enhancing productivity and making them money. Like I said earlier, when you know the answers, the questions are quite easy!

You continue to go through the feature, benefit and value of your product or service and address the way you can meet the needs that your client expressed in the needs discovery stage. For each and every feature, benefit and value presented, you then systematically confirm the connection by asking specific questions like: "IF this particular feature fills the need you expressed earlier and provides this benefit, would that be of value to you?" You need to get excited for your client as you begin to meet each need that you uncover.

Try to get prospects or clients to buy from you for their reasons. "So, IF we can get this with maroon stripes, that's the one you would prefer, is that correct?" "Now, IF we are able to get the order here for you by next Monday, that's what you would like correct?" If you're meeting or "filling" the specific needs that they have established, it's hard for them to say no to your questions. Signing the order form is just a formality, because they decided to give you the order before the paperwork was even presented.

Stage 4: CLOSING THE SALE

At this point, if you have met all the needs that you uncovered and provided the feature, benefit and value to the client, asking for the order should be academic. The client should feel very comfortable favoring you with the order, but you still have to ask, "So, when would you like this delivered?" Be known as a "closer." Good closers have good lifestyles!

The two main reasons why orders are lost are: First, when the proposal information and pricing is merely delivered or faxed accompanied by the comment, "Call me when you've had a chance to think it over." Never fax or e-mail a quote unless it's for an order confirmation. Second, sitting with prospects, handing them the proposal but never specifically asking for the order. Plain and simple, you don't get if you don't ask!

"Timid salesmen raise skinny children!"
Zig Ziglar

The secret to growing sales is to ask for the order! Be assertive, not aggressive. Consider the time that you invested in gathering the information with prospects or clients and the time to prepare the proposal. As a good businessperson, you expect to get a good return on the investments you make. A good approach to securing verbal commitment on an order is to ask for some potential dates they might expect to start doing business with you. For example: "Just to confirm, once everything is in place, would you like us to deliver these items this week or would next week be better?" This line of questioning gets you in the habit of asking direct questions that put clients in the mind-set of giving you the order. You can ask specifically, "Can you think of any reason why we wouldn't be favored for this contract?" Expect to get the order, and don't ever be afraid to ask for it. A very important thing to remember is when you're asking questions, wait for their answer. Remain silent! Resist the temptation to blurt out some kind of encouragement or ask another question. While there's power in the question, remember also that sometimes **silence is golden!**

Handling Objections

There would be a strong consensus among salespeople that objections are one of the toughest challenges for them to face! Good salespeople are always very well prepared for objections they could potentially face regarding their own product or service. Most objections that are related to a product or service are often easily and professionally answered with the feature, benefit and value approach. Other concerns or objections can be addressed by asking pointed questions to get specific answers about what their real concerns are. Uncover them, discuss them and make every attempt to resolve their issues to their satisfaction. This is where good people skills become a valuable asset to communication and influencing their choices.

A response that an inexperienced salesperson will hear frequently from clients and not handle very well is: "I would like to think it over." What clients are really saying: **"I am not convinced that you can take care of my needs."** To be optimistic, clients that would like to "think it over" may encourage you to think that they are interested. However, my experience tells me that when clients want to "think it over," that is often a delayed no! It will encourage you to know, it's also been my experience that if you consistently and systematically follow the four stages of the sales cycle, you will rarely, if ever, hear that kind of response!

If you follow the four stages of selling and meet the legitimate needs of clients, they should feel quite comfortable about giving you the order. If not, they must have a reason not to favor you. If you want the order to be yours, you must uncover what that reason is! Discuss what it will take to earn their business. If you were able to uncover and solve their objections or challenges, you have bought obligation with them to earn the order. Then ask the question, "Having eliminated this as a challenge for you, can you think of anything else that will stop us from getting started on this project?" When you handle the objection, you earn the right to ask for the order.

If they seem satisfied that you can adequately fill their needs and have answered all of their inquiries, you are now ready to get a commitment from them. I suggest requesting a purchase order, a deposit or both to secure the order. This will establish a commitment of their intention to favor you with that order. This is a good business practice and will not be an issue for clients if they are serious about you being their supplier. Those that will not commit to a purchase order or deposit, are not very serious about doing business with you or still have unresolved issues. Being highly successful in sales requires posture and an assertive attitude to ask tough questions to pursue and influence their commitment. Be determined and believe with passion that you deserve every order you go after. The client will sense that and respect it!

Body Language

When dealing with people, if you can learn to read body language, it will tell you a lot about what someone is thinking or feeling. In chapter three we glanced at some body language indicators that help us identify the personality of some people.

We actually know more about body language than we even realize. If we just think about that for a moment, we can quite easily spot someone who is angry, sad or happy. We can also spot people who are impatient, frustrated or in love. We are actually very capable at reading nonverbal communication signs if we take the time to notice them.

(+) Some very obvious positive body language includes:
Nodding in agreement, smiling, chin stroking, leaning forward index finger on the temple and note taking. These are a few sure signs you're giving someone your full attention.

(-) Some very obvious negative body language to be aware of:
Pursed lips, crossed arms, heavy sighs, rubbing eye, picking imaginary lint off one's sleeve, looking at watch or fingernails, pulling at one's collar and a full hand over the mouth. These are some of the indications that a person does not agree with you and may disapprove with what you're saying.

Body Language (continued)

In sales, these nonverbal indicators are frequently referred to as buying signs or buying signals. What prospects are feeling or thinking very often shows up on their face and/or in their movements and actions. The '**D**', '**I**', '**S**' and '**C**' personalities are also quite easy to pick up as visible body signals. For instance: What body movements would an outgoing person potentially display? Most likely energetic, quick or rough. This would identify a '**D**' or an '**I**' personality. Become good at reading these signs or signals, and you'll take an enormous step forward in becoming more influential. You may even be able to save a few orders! Key: Take the time to notice the signs!

"You're never going to get what you want in life without taking some risks."
Lee Iacocca

Selling as a profession is not for the shy and timid, because there is the potential for many forms of rejection and disappointment. However, if you can persevere and weather the storms of adversity and rejection, selling can be the most financially rewarding of all professions on the planet. If that appeals to you and gets you excited, then I say, "Go for it!" Be determined to be influential and make a difference. If you don't make a decision about what's important to you in your life, someone else may just decide for you!

Let's review some keys to selling as a profession:

Break the ice	Find the need
Build rapport	Fill the need
Build trust	Be the last presenter
Use F.O.R.M.	Ask 'IF' questions
Qualify serious buyers	Ask for the order
More calls = more sales	Handle objections
Understand body language	Silence is golden
Have an "ownership" attitude	
Ask questions that you know the answers to	

9

IN PRAISE OF PEOPLE

**A good compliment is like a full tank of gas,
you can go for miles on one.**

A compliment is a simple form of praise and recognition. If you can practice being complimentary on a regular basis, it will pay big dividends in building influence with people. It is important to be sincere and truthful when you compliment someone, and your motivation should not just be to win their favor. Proper motive and sincerity is an important consideration. If you spot people doing something nice or wearing something you appreciate, feel free to share that with them. You don't even have to know people to praise them or give them a compliment. Make a positive impact in someone's day for no other reason than – just because.

Imagine if you received a compliment from a complete stranger. How would that impact you? I really appreciate a well-dressed businessperson, and I love sharp neckties! When I am out and about and happen to see a man wearing a great tie, I will stop and tell him, "You look really sharp, and that's a great tie!" I will occasionally get a surprised look and an awkward, "Thanks," but more frequently I get an appreciative, "Why thank you." If people take the time to look good, I like to take the time to tell them that I appreciate the effort. Which tie do you think that person will select the next time he wants to impress someone?

I will never forget a compliment I once gave to a business acquaintance I admired. He always took the time to dress so well. I saw him one evening after a business function, and he was looking very sharp and professional. I said to him, "Hey Gaby, I appreciate how you always look so sharp and **that** is a really great tie!" He said, "Thanks, you really like it?" I said, "It is a very classy tie for sure." To my complete surprise, he untied it, slipped it off, folded it and gave it to me and said, "It's yours." My motivation in giving him a compliment was certainly not to obtain his tie but merely to praise his consistent effort of being well dressed.

Giving me the tie was an unselfish and genuinely friendly gesture that I didn't expect. After he gave me his tie,I said, "I really think your shoes are kind of nice too!" We had a good laugh, but I know he always appreciated my compliments. He told me that this was his way to say thanks for always taking the time to notice and make him feel good. I still have that tie today and will always keep it. It reminds me of the power of praise and the impact of a compliment. To give you some insight into his personality, he is a very reserved, people person, probably an 'S' with 'C' blend type personality. He is a really likeable and nice person, and his basic need is appreciation.

Food fills a person's stomach,
but praise fills the soul and lifts the spirit.

It's very surprising how many people do not even know how to receive a compliment. I was not used to it myself. When I was in my early twenties, someone overheard me get a compliment one day, and I didn't respond. That person was kind enough to take me aside and point out that I should have at least said, "Thank you." I was so thankful to that person I decided to marry her. I am truly grateful for that wise directive, because I now understand that compliments are hard to come by.

The practice of praising people comes in many forms. As mentioned in the first line of this chapter, a compliment is a great form of praise. Some other great praise action words are, encourage, edify, support, kindness, belief, affirm and love.

High 'I' people love getting praise! When giving praise, the high 'I' types will often be predictably loud and obnoxious but always with the best of intentions. Do something impressive, and the high 'I's' will whoop and holler up a storm to cheer you on to greater heights. You may be embarrassed to be with them when they perform their actions and antics. 'I' personalities don't really get embarrassed.

I can tell you from personal experience, high 'I' personalities don't do anything on low volume or in a reserved fashion. They like to give praise but love to get praise even more! My 'D'/'C' wife and I ('D'/'I') have four daughters that possess the 'I' personality as their highest or second highest style. A glance at our girls: #1 - 'I'/ 'S'/ 'D', #2 - 'I'/ 'S'/ 'C' #3 - 'I'/ 'S' and #4 'S'/ 'I'/'C'. Unbelievable, but true! ...and God smiles!

The personality that is often quick to praise another is the supportive 'S' person. 'S' types are amiable and want to make sure you feel good about who you are and what you do. The high 'S' types will encourage, praise and cheer you on long after everyone else has left. They easily recognize personal contribution and sacrifice and are quick to give credit where credit is due. Since both the 'I' and 'S' types are people-oriented, praise is more natural and comfortable for them. Little thought has to be put into it.

From the task side of life, the straight 'C' would feel extremely challenged praising someone simply as a spontaneous gesture just to lift a person's spirits. Only perfection is worthy of recognition for the high standards of a 'C'. High 'C' people can be so logical in their approach to life that they become critical and tend to be quite unsociable. To spontaneously praise people just to make them feel good is illogical and would make no sense to the high 'C'. When they believe a person truly deserves it, they will be able to justify offering praise to someone. They can begin to change and learn to praise by focusing on the act. Praising the act may seem easier to justify for a high 'C' personality type.

If a 'C' has a secondary 'S' or 'I' style, that person will have an easier time giving praise, but it still has to be deserved. If the secondary style is 'D', there's some work to do! Just like the high 'C' person, praise and compliments for the pure 'D' would also have to be a justified act. They expect things to be done and done with authority, period. Take charge, with no hesitation. Complete your work and feel the satisfaction of a job well done. That's your reward!

As with high 'C's', high 'D's' are not generous at giving praise. 'D's' do not easily see the purpose in praise. "Well done," coupled with a shoulder squeeze may be the only encouragement they offer for a championship win. Their daily focus is on getting things accomplished. They live to see results.

Strong 'C' and 'D' types need to learn to develop some understanding of the importance of generous praise for all the other personality types. Neglecting this motivation has the potential to not only affect their relationships but their financial status as well. Becoming more relational is an area of growth for these two types.

Praise the act not the individual!

The strategy of praising the act and not the individual accomplishes several things. It creates a strong desire in that person to repeat the action, and it also avoids potentially embarrassing the individual. It can also avoid ideas of favoritism in a group setting where others are competing for your favor and acceptance.

In her book *Silver Boxes*, author Florence Littauer writes about the power that lies in words of encouragement, praise and appreciation. The uplifting words you give to others are like giving a gift in a silver box with a blue bow on it. She encourages her readers to make small silver gift boxes with blue bows and place them in visible places around their house to remind them to encourage, praise and appreciate others.

Praise and promote in everything you do! Make an oath to praise someone at least once a day. The words you choose to speak, either positive or negative, will affect people and change lives. You get to decide! You are in control!

Parents need to take advantage of opportunities to build up and praise their children. Life is very busy and sometimes gets in the way of some of the small but important things that can make an enormous difference in the lives of those closest to us. The words of praise and encouragement that are spoken in the home are a big part of the comfort and security of children. Parents have to remember that a compliment or a word of praise must stand alone to have full impact. Often, as parents we will praise or give a compliment to our children and in the very next breath take it away by saying, "but you forgot this" or "you didn't do that!" Just as in sales, you ask the question and then remember silence is golden! You want to practice the same control when you praise your kids. Just deliver it! **Get your "but" out of the way of your praise!**

School teachers have a tremendous opportunity to praise and encourage children. School is a great place to help kids feel good about themselves and their accomplishments. Unfortunately, it can also be a place where children get set up for failure. Much has to do with the attitudes of the teacher. If teachers are wired for success, they will look to find the positive attributes in children and build on them. I can't think of a better way to start shaping young minds than to build them up with praise and appreciation. Teachers can build the belief in young people that they are special and have value.

To be positive and praise people is a decision. We have the power to choose everyday. If you make the choice to have a praise-and-promote attitude, you will be a very likeable person to be around.

Let's review some keys to praising people:

Be sincere	Be specific
Be an encourager	Edify others
Be properly motivated	Give compliments
Appreciate people's efforts	Decide to be positive
Praise the action not the person	Praise at least once a day

"Always try to bring out the best in people,
and you will be welcomed everywhere you go."

Norman Vincent Peale

10

OFFER A SKILLFUL CRITIQUE

Don't make mountains out of molehills.

I heard a story from a successful veteran retail salesperson about his early days as a very young sales clerk. He was very thankful, and he credits the wise critique of an astute leader for much of his success in the retail business. I'll call the man Frank.

Frank shared this story about the very early days of his career. The president of his company was walking the floor of his large store one morning. He noticed a customer waiting to be served at one end of a long counter while several salespeople were engaged in a social discussion at the opposite end of that same counter. Frank was one of them! The president quietly went over and served the customer himself and before finalizing the sale, he specifically selected Frank, one of the oblivious young sales clerks. After he called Frank over, the president turned to the client and said, "I will leave you in the hands of one of the brightest rising stars of our sales team to register and wrap your purchase. Thank you very much for shopping in our store today. We appreciate your business." With that, he turned away and continued his tour of the store.

The president made the sale for Frank and provided the client with the proper attention necessary. The second important thing that happened is that the president did not openly embarrass Frank. The president acted in a manner that kept resentment from developing. In fact, he paid Frank a compliment as to his future potential with the company while diplomatically establishing an expected standard for his future performance.

Later that day, the president called on the young clerk for a quick one-on-one chat. He started by thanking Frank for helping to close the sale. He also told him, "I am very thankful we have so much young talent, and I truly believe that you specifically can be a top performer for our sales team. Would you like that?" Frank replied, "Yes I would."

The president continued by saying, "In order to accomplish that, we must remember the customer is king in the retail business. We must create an environment that gives customers that idea without actually saying those words. I am sure you understand that if customers are not pleased with our service, they will stop buying, and if we have no customers, it will be tough to keep the doors open. Does that make sense to you?" "Yes, absolutely!" Frank said. His final word to Frank that day was, "I'm pleased to have you on the team and expect great things from you." The president led by example. He set an expectation for performance, initiated cooperation and finished with an upbeat and powerful message.

Frank is a high 'D' personality with a strong secondary 'I' blend. Imagine the different path his sales career and his life may have taken if the president had chosen to teach him a lesson in front of the client and his peers?

Principle: A successful critique depends on the spirit and on the timing of the delivery.

The 'D' and 'C' personality types generally have little to no problem offering a direct and unsolicited comment or critique of something someone has done. If they are not careful, they will have an inappropriate spirit in their delivery. The 'C' types with an eye for correctness can be very critical or picky with others who do not adhere to their same values. The high 'D's' will have little patience for others who don't have the drive or desire to get things done like they do. Both the 'C' and 'D' types want others to conform to their way, because their way is the right way. They can both be very direct. The high 'I's' must be aware that they also have to exercise control over what they say. They can be great encouragers but can also say things that are inappropriate and cutting in an attempt to get a laugh or be noticed. They must think before they speak. They have a unique ability to be able to apologize quickly to correct a wrong, but they must remember that sometimes words spoken in the wrong spirit can leave scars that never really heal.

The high 'S' individuals would probably be the best at offering a critique, because they would exercise the best control in terms of watching what they say so they don't offend you. The high 'S', more than anyone, is very interested in helping you and would never dream of hurting you.

You can fix the blame, or you can fix the problem. If your critique is motivated by the desire to build relationships or promote improvement, there are certain guidelines to follow that will gain a more receptive response. If you wish to tell people off or tear them down just to vent your disapproval and make yourself feel better, your comments will be sure to promote resentment.

A few guidelines to follow for a proper critique:

• Speak privately with the individual involved
• Initiate your comment with a kind word to soften the blow (Use the "sandwich approach;" say something positive, then offer the critique and close with a positive comment)
• Do not raise your voice; remain in calm and in control
• Try to criticize the act and not the person
• Provide an alternative direction, action or solution

How many times have you been told by someone that you did something well and then they said the **"but"** word? An example would be when our parents, in their attempt to get us to achieve better grades, may have said something like this, "You did great in math but had you worked harder, your English and history marks would have been better." Any initial compliment will lose its luster quite quickly in the shadow of the **"but"** remark. You did that very well, **but...**! As it was shared on page 87, get the **but** out of the way. Now, note how you can change a few words and produce a positive critique, "You did great in math and by applying that same effort in English and history next term, your marks will be where you need them to be." Here the focus is on the success that was achieved in math, and that was used as the benchmark for achievement in the other courses that need attention in the next term.

Set a standard of excellence, then work to motivate people to achieve your expectations. Never criticize anything or anyone if you cannot offer a solution to their challenge. If you are going to tell people they are doing something wrong, be prepared to tell them how do to it right.

My father-in-law U.B., as I call him, has a quality I greatly admire. He happens to be a very high 'S' personality with high 'I' and with some well-placed 'D' from time to time being Italian! He has always been able to look at a mistake or fault and find an easy way to make it right. Each time I shared a challenge with him, he gave the same confident answer. He'd say, "Hey, let's have a look, and we'll see if we can take care of that." What a great attitude! He is one of my favorite people in the world!

We have played many golf games together, and he always had a way to steer and direct me with a few gently - spoken words and a squeeze of my neck to settle me down. From the first tee to the 18th green, he would be my biggest encourager, no matter how badly I played. When things got ugly, he would wait until I was smacking shots onto every fairway other than the one I was playing on before he would point me back to the green we were supposed to be shooting for. Even when I crashed my motorcycle, he put it back together for me and never said a negative word about it. He made it into a project. He fixed it, and then he suggested I sell it and go on a golf vacation with him, so I did! A person that has the skill to critique people without offending them can make a mistake seem like no problem at all. That's Influence!

Let's review some keys to offering a skillful critique:

Stay in control, be calm   Be diplomatic
Don't raise your voice   Don't embarrass people
Be kind and considerate   Sandwich + / - / +
Seek a private place to talk   Criticize the act
See problems as opportunities
Assist them to correct the wrong
Set the standards for future performance

PRESENT WITH CONFIDENCE

**People's fear of speaking in public is greater
than their fear of dying!**

There are a number of reasons why folks do not like to speak in front of a group. People do not want to be embarrassed or appear stupid to others. They ultimately want to be accepted and appreciated no matter what personality they are blessed with. In front of a crowd, people are under the spotlight and all eyes are focused on them. People are often fearful about which personal deficiencies or limitations may become exposed to others. To simply speak in front of others is one thing, but to speak effectively and with influence is quite another. With proper instruction and training, anyone can speak like a pro. If the dream is big enough, the facts don't count!

The high 'I' personality is the most sensitive to being rejected or accepted. They love recognition and want to be the center of attention. When 'I's' speak before a crowd, their focus should be on content more than presence or enthusiasm. Staying on subject and keeping it short will be their biggest challenge. High 'I's' should try not to have too many stories and jokes and include some strong supporting facts to validate the information they are presenting.

The presentation of a high 'D' is full of confidence and power. A 'D' will give you the bottom-line answers. Alternately, a 'C' type person will give you details. The presentation of 'C' types is guaranteed to have some great nuggets of wisdom and detail. They will be factual and informative but may tend to be dull and dry. The secondary or supporting personalities for these two task-driven people will help determine the impact and effectiveness of their talks. An example would be the combination of a high 'D' with an 'I' blend. This is a strong, informative and often funny combination and usually makes for a great presenter as long as there is balance.

It's not what you have; it's what you do with what you have.

Our shy high 'S' individuals will look for ways to avoid being in front of any crowd. An audience of two people is a crowd for high 'S's'. They prefer to listen, unless they are very familiar with the other two present. Again their desire and ability to present anything will depend on the blend of their secondary personality. Remember, 'S's' make a great audience!

Here are a few basic keys to follow to become a better speaker and to present effectively to any size group. From there, it just takes practice. The more times you do it, the easier it becomes. Follow these keys, and you will be begin to be able to speak in front of any number of people without hesitation.

1. Speak from knowledge.
   - Know what you are talking about.
   - Know what you want to say. (Use 3 x 5 note cards)
   - Speak with confidence, enthusiasm and passion.
   - Provide support material to validate your presentation.

2. Speak to keep the group's interest.
   (Don't wander away from the topic.)
   - Find ways to hold their attention.
   - Use stories and personal, real-life experiences.

3. Look at your audience when you speak. (Eye contact)
   - People worth speaking to, are worth looking at.

4. Be as brief as possible, but be thorough.
   - Don't overstay your welcome.

5. Be your natural self, the real you.
   - Don't try to be someone you're not.

Some Polishing Points:

Be on time: If your event begins at 9:00, being on time is arriving a minimum of 30 - 40 minutes before the scheduled starting time. Arrive at least 1 hour prior if you have audio-visual equipment or a resource table to set up. Check that you have all that you need for the actual presentation. If you realize that you have forgotten anything, you have some time to react or improvise to correct the situation.

Be well prepared: Daniel Webster said, "No man, not inspired can make a good speech without preparation." Have your notes, support material or handouts ready and in place for when you need them. Have a podium to put your notes and support materials on. Have water nearby to help keep your vocal chords well hydrated. Know how long your talk will last.

Appropriate attire: Wear clean and pressed business dress to create a good first impression. (See chapter 3 for recommended gender specific business attire.)

Clarity: Focus on clarity. Speak clearly, at a good volume and steady pace; try not to be monotone. Try not to say non-words like "um" or anything repetitive. If a microphone is needed, be certain that it is tested and functioning properly. If you are using visual aids that require your hands often, speak with a lapel microphone to keep your hands free.

Flash a big, sincere smile: Be inviting, not intimidating. Harness the contagious power of a smile. If you look and act excited, people will respond in an exciting way. Try to remember it this way, "Thunder is good; thunder is impressive, but it's the lightning that gets the work done." -Mark Twain

Solicit feedback: Encourage attendees to give their feedback. Provide them with a quick and easy feedback questionnaire.

Some don'ts: I would advise against chewing gum or eating candy during your presentation. Try not to present with your hands in your pockets or playing with coins. I also recommend not using off-color or inappropriate humor at any time.

Let's review some keys to presenting with confidence:

Be on time (30 minutes early)	Flash a smile
Dress for success	Be well - prepared
Be you, not somebody else	Look at people
Keep your hands out of your pockets	Speak with clarity
No off-color or inappropriate humor	No gum or mints

"Perseverance is consistency under pressure.
Perseverance gives a person the strength and a resolve
to accept whatever comes, to face life head-on
and to stand firm."

Dick DeVos

12

SHOW APPRECIATION AND GRATITUDE

Human nature tells us that people respond favorably to those who show them genuine appreciation and gratitude. Just a simple thank you can go a long way. I remember as a young boy when our family would go to a relative's house or out in public, my mom would say, "Now kids, you be sure to mind your manners. Say, 'Yes please and no thank you,' understand?" We were also frequently told, "If you don't appreciate what you have, you won't get anything else." It really comes down to personal training. Being thankful is an attitude.

The 'S' and 'I' type personalities may find the practice of showing appreciation and gratitude easier, because they are more people-oriented. The 'S' person loves to be appreciated and the 'I' type person loves to be recognized. Showing appreciation and gratitude for the 'S' and 'I' person is part of their basic wiring and is a normal everyday function for them. It is not something they really have to work at very hard.

The dominant, high 'D' and cautious, high 'C' types will have a greater challenge in this area because of the emphasis that they place on tasks. They focus on completing tasks not on relating to people. They generally believe that accomplishment is its own reward; therefore, things do not need to be done with fanfare.

Typically, people will communicate in the same "language" that they themselves would respond to when they deal with others. If they communicate with a certain style, they feel others should respond favorably to that same style also. This is not a proper assumption, but seems to be a fairly consistent mind-set when it comes to communication. This is a good basic understanding to be aware of when dealing with people, because it will heighten awareness of people's tendencies and can establish a healthy climate for initiating relationships. This is why we don't always relate to everyone, because everyone is quite different. When you do happen to find someone that responds to your communication style, you connect.

You really have to make a decision every day to be thankful for the things you receive and for the things that happen to you. If you start feeling that you have a right to have all things the way you want them, you become guided by self-interest. My grandfather once told me, "You came into the world naked and that's how you'll leave, so be thankful for all the things that you earn and doubly thankful for the things that are given to you. You get out of life what you put into it; put nothing into it, and that's what you'll get back - nothing."

"Have an attitude of gratitude."
Zig Ziglar

If you show people that you are grateful and that you appreciate them, they will continue to come around. If you are not willing to show and tell people that you are thankful, there may never be another opportunity. People know when you appreciate them. It will show in your actions as well as in your words.

Principle: Show others the measure of appreciation and gratitude you expect to have shown in return.

Be sincere when being thankful and look directly at the person you thank. Be sure that you communicate clearly and distinctly regarding what you appreciate, and why you want to show your gratitude towards them.

If you can take notice of the finer things that often go unnoticed and recognize them with appreciation, this will distance you from the average person. Many people are superficial. It takes a special person to see details that others may not appreciate. Go the extra mile to appreciate.

Take an inventory in your life. Write down a list of all the things that you appreciate and are truly thankful for. Family, friends and health usually top the list. Material possessions are not what we value and appreciate the most. We must remember to remind ourselves of this as often as we can!

We must remember that our life is made up of many contributions and influences. No one person is self-made. Parents, grandparents, siblings, teachers, friends, acquaintances and even our adversaries have made both positive and negative deposits in our lives. All of these things together help form us into the people we are. People do not naturally do kind and helpful things for others. It comes down to making a choice! Ultimately, we are responsible to make our own decisions regarding our attitude and approach to life. The circumstances we daily experience will influence our attitudes and decisions. We can appreciate and be thankful for the things that happen to us and decide to have a good attitude, or we can have a bad attitude and live upset and miserable lives. This will certainly affect our attitude towards others. I choose to see the cup as half full and not half empty!

When someone believes in something, they make an investment in the hopes of getting a return. In the same way, if people invest in other people, it's because they believe in them. Showing appreciation and gratitude is a simple but great return for that investment. Often we don't really appreciate the investment that others have made and continue to make in us.

While we may be wired in a certain way, that doesn't mean we cannot change and grow to become a person that takes time to be thankful and appreciative. Look at who you have become and remember who and what has helped shape the person that you are. Give thanks and appreciate the people and the life experiences you have enjoyed so far. Dream big dreams and set goals to make something of yourself. Along the way, have an attitude of gratitude.

Let's review some keys to show appreciation and gratitude:

Be grateful   Be sincere
Say thank you and mean it   Be clear and distinct
Make a daily decision to be thankful
Understand that we are not self-made
Give back a good return on a person's investment in you

"Success comes from having the proper aim
as well as the right ammunition."

Author unknown

13

LEADERSHIP AND INFLUENCE

"The true measure of leadership is influence, nothing more, nothing less." *John C. Maxwell*

Leadership is a diverse and multifaceted subject that has inspired many great books. There are many different leadership models, approaches and theories. In this chapter, I will share what I believe to be true about influence and its connection to leadership.

I believe that the effectiveness of a leader will depend largely on the degree of influence and hope he or she gives to others. John Maxwell's quote seems to support that belief. We must also remember that, we cannot fix other people; we can only fix ourselves. A leader that desires to influence people must seek to provide an environment that stimulates growth and motivates a person to be influenced to change for the better.

We choose and decide to do things hundreds of times each day. We cannot escape it! We ask ourselves things like, "Does that make me happy or sad? Should I rush or take my time?" Those are simple choices that we don't think about for very long. Other more difficult choices require considerably more thought. With the choices and decisions that we make, we shape our lives and the world around us. Change happens when choices are made! We as leaders cannot choose for others. If people decide to change as a result of our influence, that's great! In the end, the choice is still theirs to make.

How often do the words that others say, influence our choices and actions? This is where I believe influence connects with leadership. The position a leader holds will often give authority or credibility to the words he or she speaks. Our words can be motivational and encouraging, and they can also be negative and destructive. The words of a leader may impact people in such a way that they will influence them to choose a path that leads to great success. Alternately, their words, if negative could also potentially hold them back from becoming all they can be.

Give people hope, and they will follow you.

Words are not the only form of influence we use. Leaders can be influential by virtue of their position and the authority that is connected to it. Often, leaders will misuse the power of their position to intimidate people into action or change. Good leaders will use their position to motivate and inspire others to become part of their vision. People will follow if they feel they will be well rewarded for their contributions.

Some people will be selected and placed in a leadership role as a result of their productive accomplishments. The hope is that they will serve as a good role model. This is a practice followed by many organizations, but it has limitations! While the success of high productivity is worthy of recognition, a quick promotion to manage others is not always the wisest, most strategic way to stimulate ongoing, productive growth.

Consistent productivity comes from developed skills and focused persistence. These are great attributes, but they are not the sole criteria used to gain respect as an influential leader. Without developing team building and effective communication skills, progress and growth are greatly minimized. Some of the greatest producers have not always been the best leaders and some very effective leaders were not always the top producers. Their skill must be shared and developed in others so that it will sustain future growth. It takes time to cultivate and develop a leader that will be able to duplicate and multiply their personal productive success.

As a leader, to be able to "talk the talk" and also "walk the walk" is important. These combine for a powerful and influential impact. Education and knowledge are valuable foundational leadership assets. I believe that knowledge gained from experience, coupled with the ability to effectively communicate has an even greater value! As a hockey instructor/coach, I share this from personal experience. I have worked hundreds of hours in arenas instructing hockey players of all ages. With the ability to both show *and* tell players what they had to do on the ice, I found that I was able to greatly influence consistent, positive results. The age or skill level was not a factor in determining the outcome with this style of instruction. Allow me to clarify. When I explain a drill without diagramming it for the players, only 50 percent of them were able to go and do it. If I took the time to diagram the drill and explain it, 80 percent of the players were able to do it. When I took the time to diagram the drill, then, demonstrate the drill by skating it through myself, 100 percent of the players were able to duplicate the drill perfectly. The skill and ability to demonstrate the proper way to do the drill made the verbal instruction much clearer and actually saved time, because it eliminated the risk of potentially having to stop the drill and re-explain it. Experience is priceless!

Leadership is a developed skill, not an appointed title.

Everyone has leadership qualities within his or her personality, because influence comes in many forms. It is often said that the success of a leader will depend largely on the kind of people that the leader surrounds himself or herself with. Teamwork is all about collective effort! One workhorse can pull a thousand pounds, but two workhorses hitched together, can pull up to four times that weight! The collective influence we can have as a team of people is amazing. Regardless of our personality, we have the potential to influence a choice every time we speak with others. So, think before you speak!

A visionary leader is always on the lookout for other potential leaders. That person will attempt to influence, encourage and cultivate others on the team to aspire to a leadership role. Wise leaders will carefully and strategically delegate responsibilities to those people that show leadership potential. They look for strengths in individuals they believe will inspire, influence and encourage others into action.

Leading according to people's strengths and potential influence is where the understanding of personalities and their tendencies becomes a tremendous asset for any leader. Throughout the book and specifically in the first chapter, this book highlights the traits of the 'D', 'I', 'S' and 'C' personalities. From this, we know who is more appropriately wired for each kind of leadership. There is an outgoing leadership style and a reserved leadership style. One, is not any better than the other. Each has positive ways to influence others. Each has good traits to bring to a leadership position.

The high 'I' or the high 'S' personality types may not be our first choice to lead an army into battle or orchestrate a corporate takeover. Much would depend on their secondary personality blend to determine their potential in an assertive leadership situation. As leaders, they would be wise to strategically select a dominant 'D' or competent 'C' to be employed in senior positions to take charge, supply direction, and organize their effort to complement their easygoing nature. Their influence comes from their strength in building rapport and relationships. Remember, they are people-oriented!

The high 'C' and more specifically the high 'D' prefers to be leading rather than being led. The 'D' usually has vision beyond what most people can understand. They can sometimes see things so big that it will scare others! They are comfortable when they're directing the action. High 'D's' lead with authority and can be counted on to complete the task they set out to achieve. Be aware, they can be quite forceful and intimidating. If you like to win, follow the 'D'!

As a leader, the critical thinking high 'C' person will run a tight ship! They will have a specific plan of action and put the proper people in place to ensure that every detail of their policies and procedures are followed to the letter. High 'C' types are extremely competent leaders but tend to be hard and inflexible. Everything is by the book. They expect perfection! The 'C' and 'D' personalities influence others by earning respect through their competence and accomplishments. Remember, they are task-oriented!

To direct and lead the high 'S' and high 'I' personalities, a leader must help them feel good and comfortable about their reasons for following them. The 'S' and 'I' types would prefer to connect with their leaders on a personal level, not only on a "strictly business" level. If a leader can relate to their easy-going perspectives and see how they see things, they will have tremendous influence to lead them. If any leader can keep it exciting and fun to stimulate the high 'I' and provide a stable, no surprises workplace for the high 'S', that leader they will have them as lifetime team players. The high 'I' craves stimulation and 'S' types are very loyal supporters.

High 'C's' will not be comfortable taking part in any project in which they were not provided a detailed job description of their role and what is to be expected of them. Defined objectives need to be outlined. To influence results with 'C's', remember that they like to have structure and predictability. If a leader can create this kind of environment for them to operate in, the 'C' personality will consistently produce and be a tremendous asset to the organization.

High 'C's' are also great support people for a leader who lacks focus and has organizational deficiencies. If a leader delegates the organizational or administrative duties of his or her team to a high 'C', that leader will have the individual who is best suited for that kind of role. It shall be done right or not done at all!

To lead and influence the dynamic 'D' personality to productivity, leaders must recognize the true value of who they have on their team. Opportunities need to be provided for high 'D's' to exercise their determined drive and need for accomplishment. Give them a role of responsibility but keep them accountable. If you can influence 'D's' to take ownership within your ranks, you will have great supporters and producers. Allow the eagles to fly and do not try to cage them up.

As a leader, it is important to position your people to maximize the strengths of as many of the personalities as you can. They will respond positively, respect you and serve you well as a leader. Know your players!

105

Good leadership is often just common sense! I have heard it said that, "Common sense isn't so common anymore." Leadership calls for leaders to make tough decisions and for that, you need wisdom, patience, discipline and sacrifice.

Wisdom is seeing the value in the right choice and understanding the potential impact and influence of that choice on the future.
Patience is knowing when to have courage and confidence in your skills and abilities. Patience is seeing the vision that removes all fear and risk from any decisions to be made for others to follow.
Discipline is deciding to do something that we wouldn't normally or typically do and seeing it through to completion.
Sacrifice is always putting the needs and desires of others before your own.

People who will take the time to invest in themselves to become this type of person, will by virtue of these skills, become a leader. Good leaders lead people by having them believe wholeheartedly that you're serving them and leading them based on their ambitions, goals and desires, not yours! With this focus, you will naturally influence and lead. Leadership and influence are by-products of developing good people skills. Help people become something they never thought they could become. That's influence and...

...Influence is the essence of leadership!

Principle: Influence and empower people to make choices based on good information.

Let's review some keys to leadership and influence:

We cannot fix others   Think before you speak
We can only fix ourselves   Influence positive choice
Create environments for growth
Look for and cultivate potential leaders
Don't just "talk the talk" but "walk the walk"

14

CONCLUSION

**Positive thinking is the hope that you can move mountains.
Positive believing is the same hope but,
with a reason for believing you can.**

No one on the planet has all the answers to all of life's situations, so we must persevere and make it through life the best way we know how. Give thanks and praise to those who want to invest in you with their love and their experience. To complement this, you should also be diligent to be influenced by people who have skills and attitudes that you want to incorporate into your life. Observe successful people, and study their success patterns. If the results they achieve are what you seek, then follow what they do and try to think the way they think. Aspire to greatness and excellence. If you cannot find someone to mentor you, look towards printed and recorded materials that can assist you to become all that God intended you to be. If you decide that you want success, then you must prepare yourself for it.

Success comes when opportunity meets with preparation.

Study and learn your personal tendencies in order to improve your relationships with others. Decide to make a positive impact on everyone around you. Remember, the people you associate with and the personal development books you read will help shape the person you become. The average person does not read one book a year. That's why they're average! Readers are leaders! You are what you read and who you associate with, so be very selective with both those choices.

I challenge you to set a standard of excellence in your life, and learn the skills it takes to make friends and be a positive influence with people. If you learn to focus on the well-being of others first, they will want to spend time with you wherever you go. You will be on your way to becoming...A Person of Influence.

Go for excellence, and God bless you!

15

THE PRINCIPLE COLLECTION

"Do you know someone you think you can change, regulate or improve? Fine. Why not start on yourself? That's a lot more profitable than trying to improve others." - *Dale Carnegie*

Principle: Understand that we are all different with a purpose.

Principle: Learn to be more observant.

Principle: Listen twice as much as you speak.

Principle: People will like you, if you make them feel important.

Principle: Catch people doing good things and compliment them.

Principle: Get others saying, "Yes, yes," as soon as possible.

Principle: "You can have everything out of life that you want if you will just help enough other people get what they want out of life."- *Zig Ziglar*

Principle: A successful critique depends on the spirit and the timing of the delivery.

Principle: Show others the measure of appreciation and gratitude you expect to have shown in return.

Principle: Influence and empower people to make choices based on good information.

To have Gordon MacFarlane present a key-note address, facilitate a training seminar or provide a personality profile assessment for you or your organization please contact:

ROMAC Communications
GROWING PEOPLE THROUGH EMPOWERMENT
Huntsville, Alabama
romac1@bellsouth.net

In Association with:

Personality Insights Incorporated
Atlanta Georgia